WALKING WITH
GIANTS

THE NEW TESTAMENT FLESHED OUT
THROUGH 20 ASIAN SERVANTS OF GOD

HARRY T. BUSH

 COURIER PUBLISHING

Greenville, South Carolina

PUBLISHED IN THE UNITED STATES OF AMERICA

ENDORSEMENTS

In President Kennedy's Pulitzer Prize book, *Profiles in Courage,* he said, "A man does what he must in spite of personal consequences, in spite of obstacles and dangers or pressures ... and that is the basis of all human morality."

Author Harry Bush takes us on a journey with a band of men and women who took the good news of Jesus into areas and situations where angels fear to tread. As I read these pages, I felt that somehow an Indiana Jones movie transcript had been transposed onto my material! This is a *must read* for every Christian living out their faith in a dangerous, unfriendly world. You may find yourself as a chapter in God's own "Profiles in Courage."

Jim Henry
Pastor Emeritus, First Baptist Church of Orlando, Florida
President Emeritus of the Southern Baptist Convention

When I first met Harry and Barbara Bush while still new missionaries, I was quickly impressed by two qualities exemplified in their lives and words. Passion and wisdom! So I was thrilled to hear about this book describing their experiences and the amazing local leaders God is raising up across Asia. Passion and wisdom! All believers will be encouraged to know about the courageous lives and ministries of such men and women. I pray that God will also call out other "sent ones" like Harry and Barbara to continue such a ministry of equipping to those who are turning the world upside down.

Don Dent
Director, Kim School of Global Missions
Gateway Seminary, Southern Baptist Convention

The same Holy Spirit who shook the world in the book of Acts is still at work in the world today. Here are stories of a modern Aquila and Priscilla who served alongside some modern Apostles, sharing the Gospel and watching God move powerfully. Open the pages and listen to some of the best stories gathered from over thirty years of serving in some of the most remote regions of the world.

E. Randolph Richards
Provost and Professor of Biblical Studies
Palm Beach Atlantic University
Coauthor of Misreading Scripture with Western Eyes

"It takes one to know one." Harry Bush recognizes missional spiritual giants because he is one. God's Spirit has been upon Harry and Barbara throughout their thirty-one years of effective mission service. With passion and compassion they have presented the claims of Christ in some of the most remote places on our planet.

With a down-to-earth style, Harry introduces us to twenty national "Spiritual Giants." Amidst spartan living conditions, Harry challenges us to sacrificial service as he relates how these national leader-giants have punched holes of Light into the walls of spiritual darkness in South and Southeast Asia.

Bill Curl, Pastoral Care
First Baptist Church/Orlando, Florida
International Mission Board Missionary Emeritus

DEDICATED TO:

BARBARA ...

My soulmate ... my wife ... my best friend, who has walked beside me in all of these experiences and 55 years of my life. Without you, there would have been no book written on pages or in our hearts. Your corrective nozzle on the end of my "word-hose" has produced a book of beautiful lives reflecting His Glory on every page. I am/we all are deeply indebted to you for doing that.

ACKNOWLEDGEMENTS

To Russell Rankin:

For the incredible job of editing this book. It could not have been accomplished without your skill and tenacity in guiding and encouraging me.

To Holly Sroka:

The Resident Life Facilitator of Westminster Manor where Barbara and I live, who started a Writer's Group that kick-started this whole project. Forever thank you.

To Bob Lauer and Taylor Hill:

Who became my "tormentors" by red-lining every misspelled word and clumsy sentence on every line of every page. These, my Confidant Readers, have shoved this book toward excellence. I am forever grateful to you both.

To Phyllis Musgrave:

Who did the labor of love to save and organize into huge albums every piece of correspondence from us, either handwritten or typed, from 1973 till 2003. Most of the detailed flavor in the book came from these "captured moments" of yesteryear and all because of your diligent love for us and your Lord.

To Michael Gunter:

My SON-in-love, author of six excellent books and minister extraordinaire, for your gentle shoves and genuine encouragement to persevere. It was needed and deeply appreciated.

To Jim and Kaye Oakley:

For the use of your beautiful house on the top of one of North Carolina's finest peaks where I was able to write the first three chapters.

To Dr. Sam Raines, Pastor of West Bradenton Baptist Church, and all of the members of that church:

Who allowed me to use a room in your church building to write this book every week for almost one year. Your gracious offer allowed me to write in silence and comfort. Thank you.

TABLE OF CONTENTS

FOREWORD

Western Christians often succumb to the perception that they possess a superior faith and understanding of the Christian life. After all, we have a rich Christian history and have been nurtured in church for multiple generations. Having such experience and biblical knowledge, it is our responsibility to take the gospel to less fortunate and spiritually deprived people around the world.

Missionaries are often put on a pedestal and considered in a special category of Christians due to their sacrifice and dedication. But any perceived echelon of spiritual distinction pales in comparison to the saintly servants of God found among national believers in India and around the world. I walked with reverent awe in the steps of saintly men like Gnaniah, a village evangelist who was beaten for his witness yet persisted until churches were planted among pagan villagers. I sat cross-legged all day long on hard, dirt floors as Pastor Solomon Raj led Bible studies that continued into the night due to people's hunger for the Word of God. I often nodded off to sleep as they prevailed in prayer, pouring out their hearts to God for their people, hour after hour.

On my frequent assignments to India, I met illiterate village workers who used their knowledge of four or five languages to take the gospel to unreached people groups. There were those who turned their backs on lucrative professions in order to share the gospel and train others. They were rejected by their families, eschewed basic comforts, and bore scars from attacks and riots for the sake of the gospel.

My life was never the same after knowing and walking alongside Stephen as he planted churches in the slums of Mumbai where the stench and poverty would have deterred others. Paul Prodhan, a simple farmer-evangelist, became esteemed like a biblical patriarch in my eyes as I saw him nurture a movement among tribal Christians in Orissa. Western

Christians look with admiration on prominent preachers and renowned leaders but are deprived of knowing such real spiritual giants whose lives are characterized by extraordinary devotion, uncompromising sacrifice and an intimate walk with God.

Readers of *Walking with Giants* have an opportunity to meet these giants and others, such as Pastor G. Samuel who trained laymen in his Hyderabad megachurch to start hundreds of churches, and Nazir Masih who led a church planting movement in the midst of Hindu radicalism in North India.

For years, Harry and Barbara Bush immersed themselves in the remote areas of India and South Asia as part of an itinerant missionary team seeking to train thousands of grassroots workers to reach into the darkness across this subcontinent. But instead of coming with all the answers from years of experience and education, they encountered giants in the land. Not Goliath-like giants who stood against the gospel as a formidable adversary, but spiritual giants God was using so that the kingdoms of this world might become the kingdoms of our Lord. I am confident this book will challenge you to a deeper dimension of spiritual growth. Pastors will find an abundance of powerful real-life testimonies to inspire their congregation. And for those considering involvement in missions, Walking with Giants will strengthen your resolve to be obedient to God's call.

The lives and ministry of the Bushes, and others on that itinerant team, will never be the same. And neither will yours as you read of the austere lifestyle, demanding travel, and cost of getting the gospel to the ends of the earth. Your heart will be broken as you read of suffering and sacrifice; you will yearn to grow in the depth of faith that characterized these giants, and will find yourself praying that, like them, you would be counted worthy to suffer for sake of Christ and His kingdom.

Jerry Rankin, President Emeritus
International Mission Board, SBC

Prologue

Important information that will help you understand the rest of this book:

Understanding the LEAD (Leadership, Equipping, And Development) ministry will greatly help you appreciate and understand the framework of the following twenty Spiritual Giants described in Walking with Giants. The LEAD ministry of the International Mission Board of the Southern Baptist Convention was a church leadership development ministry created for uneducated and undereducated pastors, church planters, and primary church leaders living in inner-city slums, impoverished rural burgs, beside jungle rivers, and atop the world's highest mountains of eleven Asian nations. Each of these twenty Giants of the faith described in this book were strengthen by this LEAD ministry.

During the time my wife Barbara and I served, the LEAD team consisted of up to seven couples traveling to more than fifty groups located throughout these Asian countries. The LEAD team's goal was to teach God's Word, spiritual truths, and biblical disciplines in an effective, simple manner so each participant could gain enough in each seminar to grow toward their fullest potential as God's servant. Many did just that, as exampled in the following accounts of the twenty selected Giants encountered through that ministry.

If you are picking up this book expecting the typical missionary biography, you will be disappointed. This is not about me or the others who served on the team with us. This book is written in honor of the great men and women we encountered during our service with LEAD, who serve their Lord bravely and selflessly in spiritually difficult and dangerous terrains. Yes, you will receive a dose of our personal narrative, as each chapter includes sections on "Getting There" and "Being There." Despite serving most of our adult lives in Asia, getting to and surviving in "the uttermost" to reach our Giants had its challenges.

The structure of the LEAD ministry was to teach each group of church leaders two times a year in five-day seminars. Each seminar consisted of two curriculum subjects and one book of the Bible taught for thirty hours from Monday through Friday. These seminars were planned for a six-year cycle which yielded learning from twenty-four subjects and twelve books of the Bible. These subjects included titles such as: The Doctrine of God, How to Teach the Bible, Spiritual Disciplines, Doctrine of Salvation, How to Plant a Church, How to Prepare a Sermon, and many more. These subjects and Bible books were taught through an interactive method that assisted the participants in remembering and being able to reteach some of everything they learned. After all, most of these leaders served in remote and often impoverished communities among people with limited education. The importance of teaching to oral cultures was critical. The participants became more productive in their ministry roles. After three years, the churches of these leaders experienced a growth ratio, on the average, of 23 percent per year.

Barbara and I were blessed to be a part of the LEAD ministry for sixteen years and direct it for ten years. Our hearts melded with these precious leaders and soared with each of their victories. In fact, we all became family; members of God's family which provided us with a little taste of heaven.

Harry T. Bush

WALKING WITH
GIANTS

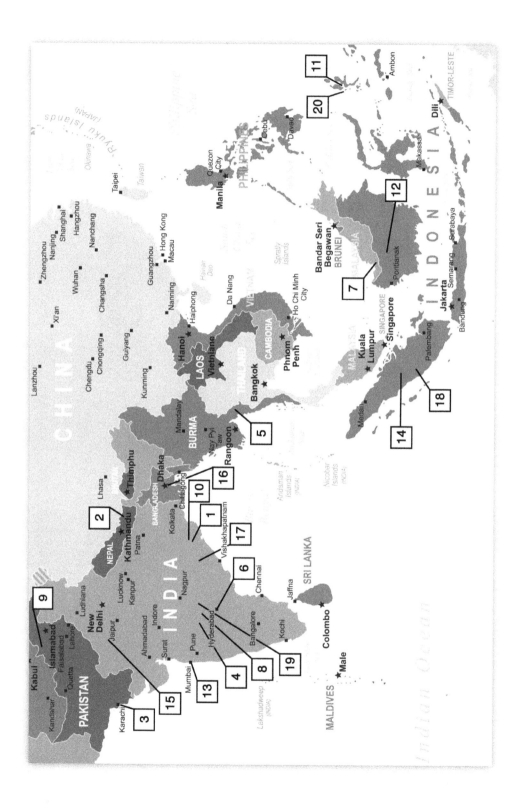

TITLES, NAMES AND PLACES OF THE TWENTY GIANTS

1. **The Farmer's Pastor:** Pastor Sudansu, Raipada, India

2. **The Himalayan Walker:** Bai Ratna Rai, Itahari, E. Nepal

3. **The Heart and Tongue of an Evangel:** Naveed Malik, Karachi, Paktistan

4. **A Small Man with a Big Heart:** Pastor Veerna, Parlekemundi, India

5. **A Burmese Giant in the Teakwood Forest:** Thra Simon, Burma/Myanmar (refugee camp in W. Thailand)

6. **The Mega-Giant of Hyderabad:** Pastor G. Samuel, Hyderabad, India

7. **Down the River to Five Hundred Years Ago:** Jackson and Seria, Sri Aman, Borneo, E. Malaysia

8. **The Life-Lifting Giants:** Adam and Eliah, Visweswarayapurim, India

9. **Heart-Shapers in a Hard Land:** Ifrahim/Matthew, Islamabad, Pakistan

10. **An Honored Giant of the Hills:** Pastor and Mrs. Paul Prodham, Mallikapuri, India

11. **The Seaside Nurturers:** Martin and Femy Adaling, Tobelo, Halmahera, Indonesia

12. **The Giant's Giant:** Pastor Ajen, Karangan, Kalimantan, Indonesia

13. **A Giant in the Slums:** Pastor Stephen, Mumbai, India

14. **A Leader's Giant:** Pastor Abu, Pekanbaru, Sumatra, Indonesia

15. **The Mustard-Seed Giant:** Pastor Nazir Masih, Chandigarh, India

16. **The Turncoat Who Turns Hearts:** Pastor Saleem, Dhaka, Bangladesh

17. **A Beautiful Man in a Beautiful Land:** Pastor and Mrs. Wayne Joseph, Araku Valley and Visakhapatnam, India

18. **A Humble Giant of the Plantation:** Pastor and Mrs. Yohanes, Muko-Muko, W. Sumatra, Indonesia

19. **The Brown Angel with Grit:** Pastor and Mrs. Jacob, Bandarigudem, India

20. **The Overcoming Giants:** Pastor Joiy and Ella Lempas, Ternate, Indonesia

1

THE FARMER'S PASTOR

Rev. Sudansu Naik could have pastored in any of the more modern, large cities in the state of Orissa, India. He had the theological credentials to do so, but he chose a different pathway. Brother Sudansu's heart was firmly rooted in the Khond Hills of Orissa with the Kui People who lived in that area. Orissa, being the state lowest on the socioeconomic ladder in India, had many serious needs, but the need for food was the most severe. The Kui of the Khond Hills were the most impoverished among all other people groups in Orissa. Many Kui died of hunger during the dry season when water was not available. In fact, in the Kui dialect, the word for "hunger," and the word for "dry season" are the same. Sudansu begged God for a solution and surrendered himself to be a part of His answer to that desperate need.

Rev. Sudansu was certain that the gospel had a major role to play in meeting both the physical needs of the Kui along with their gigantic spiritual ones. After all, he had married Paul Prodhan's daughter (see chapter 8: "An Honored Giant of the Hills"), so he had a bird's-eye view of just how powerful the gospel was. He had observed the miraculous changes in individuals, families, and whole communities as a result of the gospel. Sudansu also knew that new farming methods would have to play an integral role if more food was to be produced. The thing he did not understand was the explosive affect, for good, that happened when two elements were combined: The gospel being melded with transformative ideas about what, how, and when to plant. This changed the lives of thousands and thousands of Kui.

In past times, God was not taxed to precisely arrange and align heavenly bodies in order to create the earth's ability to produce life and sustain it. Therefore, in the present, neither was He challenged to align choice servants to meet the needs of the Kui, and others far beyond the Khond Hills. God moved Jerry Rankin and Fred Beck to direct some of His work in India for Southern Baptists. Then He led Fred to link arms with Dr. Patra of Orissa, a professor in the Indian Forestry Ministry. Together they formulated an experimental agricultural program for the Khond Hills. John Langston was also moved like a chess piece into an important position to flesh out this program. Afterwards, God selected two of His finest servants from the Philippines, Calvin and Margaret Fox, to be the on-the-ground progenitors of the Rural Life Development Foundation in India. Working with Dr. Patra, they created an experimental farm in Raipada, India. The Farm, as it was called, became the "Hand of God" which delivered masses of the Kui people from serious starvation during the ensuing dry seasons.

One of Calvin's first choices was the selection of Pastor Sudansu, who helped develop the spiritual import to the farmers and students who came to the Farm. It was the combination of these Indian and American leaders applying muscle and sweat to the gospel that changed the definition of the word for "dry season." It took years of teaching and applying these truths before that starvation rate among the Kui became almost nil, but it did happen. "Dry season" no longer meant "hunger."

For instance, when Brother Pitobas Digal first attended the Farm, he did not know who Jesus Christ was. He had lost a baby and his father in the previous hunger/dry season. He was young and desperate. Brother Sudansu taught him a series of chronological Bible stories. This method fit well with the way truths were shared in the Kui communities. After the powerful stories of the crucifixion and resurrection, Pitobas received Jesus as his personal Savior. Since he was in the three-month short program at the Farm, he received less instruction on what to plant, when to plant, and how to plant it. However, with what Pitobas received he was able to be significantly more productive with his crops. He also absorbed some teachings on community healthcare from a marvelous doctor and his wife whom Calvin and Margaret enticed into the Rural Development Program. Dr. Sanjeev Seelam and his capable nurse/wife produced astounding results in that program. They were both believers and took that task on as their life's mission. They would go out to the Kui communities on weekends and do health clinics among the villages where graduates of the Rural Life Program lived and worked.

One of the first things Pitobas did when he returned back home was to move the outhouse far away from the shallow well that served a number of families in his village. He taught his family to take daily baths and wash their hands before handling any food. He showed them where to find some plants in the forest that would help heal cuts, bring down fevers, or even aid in healing their coughs. These helps alone quickly translated into more healthy lives for his family and neighbors. It drew attention like a neon sign. During those same three months Brother Sudansu taught Pitobas a number of important Bible stories. Pitobas learned how to repeat them so he would not forget them. He learned to pray and depend on Almighty God. He was beginning to walk daily with Jesus. Sudansu waited for Pitobas to return to his village in order to baptize him in his own community. It was a testimony to his neighbors about the Source of all of the blessings they were seeing with their own eyes.

Because of genuine witnesses like Pitobas, many house churches started to appear up and down the hills and throughout the tree-car-peted valleys like stars of an early night sky. Those graduates of the Farm had returned to their villages with not only new farming techniques but also with new lives that reflected their newly found hope in Jesus. Transformation took shape more rapidly than anyone had thought possible. In the daytime at the Farm, Pastor Sudansu taught chronological Bible storying, and how to teach it to others. Often at night, he helped groups in the surrounding villages to develop into New Testament churches. He was a genuine Giant!

Another example from the Rural Development Life Center was Basudeb Pathmaibi. He was a Kui from a village far away from the Farm, but had heard some remarkable stories about it. He just showed up one day and would not go away. He also was desperate. Sudansu finally got him enrolled into the nine-month long program. Basudeb was trying to hold onto his family's land, but was losing the battle. They just could not turn a profit. Every health crisis, poor crop production and, not to mention, his gambling efforts, set them back farther.

In a shockingly short time, Basudeb received Christ. Since he could already read, Sudansu not only taught him Bible stories, but gave him a Bible which Basudeb began to read immediately. Clearly, he had an aptitude for spiritual things and grew rapidly in his early Christian life. At the same time he was absorbing the farming techniques and methodology. Basudeb latched onto Calvin's "off-season food and cash crop" lessons concerning the planting and harvesting of bamboo. Bamboo is a real money crop in Orissa because every building project, house or building requires loads of bamboo. Calvin had developed a method for growing bamboo twice as fast as the normal time. The sugarplum on top of it all was that bamboo could be grown on any terrain, not necessarily taking up vital crop-growing space. This development alone may have saved a huge portion of Kui farmers from financial ruin. Basudeb utilized this bamboo technique to quickly pay off his debts and even was able to expand his land holdings. He also became a lay-pastor under Sudansu's steady hand and led a church to grow into a strong congregation.

God's great results with the Kui were shouldered by many Giants, all pulling together in one accord for His honor. Each one was indispensable, especially Calvin and Margaret Fox. However, it was Calvin who had God's eyesight when he secured Brother Sudansu Naik to be the "gospel-glue" that fastened many of students at the Farm to the Lord Jesus Christ. It was Sudansu who watered and fertilized these young souls into becoming lay-pastors and church planters at the same time that they were profitable farmers. When Sudansu arrives at heaven's gate there will be a mass of former Kui to meet him. They will be singing, clapping, and giving joyous shouts to the Lord God because of the faithfulness of this farmer's pastor.

Barbara and I were always blessed when we stood beside Pastor Sudansu, whether in a formal class setting as he translated our materials, or at night when we saw him encouraging some of the under-educated farmers with their homework assignments. Sudansu constantly challenged us by his servant attitude. He never stopped encouraging one Kui to go to another Kui with the gospel that opened the door of joyous living here on earth and guaranteed them eternal life in heaven. He was a true Giant.

GETTING THERE

Traveling to Raipada up in the Khond Hills of Orissa is a carbon copy of the trip to Mallikapuri described in chapter 8, as they are only about ten miles apart. We flew into Bhubaneswar, the capital city of Orissa, where we overnighted in the New Kenilworth Hotel. We were transported to Raipada, the Farm, in a car by the same company that drove us to Mallikapuri. The trip normally took about five hours or longer, according to whether the driver got lost or not. Life was framed by the car windows as we drove along the two-lane paved road. Some of the framed pictures broke my heart.

I saw a young boy perched high up on a stack of straw that filled a wooden wagon moving slowly down the side of the road. He only wore a colorless pair of shorts. His super-tanned body spoke of hours in the scalding sunlight. The wagon lurched behind a large, rib-showing, Brahma bull, as he plodded down the road. My first impression was, "Poor lad. Life's going to get a lot harder for you." But then, on second reflection, he was on a wagon, pulled by a working animal, hauling a large amount of straw left over from harvesting a big rice field. No, this boy probably came from a family who owned things. He had a name; maybe even a future. But, was anyone caring for his soul?

Not long after we passed that wagon and started up the slope into the Khond Hills, another picture was caught through the window. Two sisters were sitting near the road on the edge of a neatly swept dirt yard. Their dirty, ragged clothes, uncombed hair, and large dark eyes, accented by their thin cheeks indicated they were imprisoned in poverty. The mud hovel, with its thatched roof, added to the possibility that these girls were of the low caste, or even no caste. That meant that they could never go into a neighbor's house if that neighbor held position in a caste. The iron jaws of the caste system locked them into the lowest rung of human existence in India. These girls would not be afforded medium to higher education, nor would they ever be able to go into a hospital or have regular health services. If they were violated there would be no police report, and certainly no justice rendered. These two, and the millions they represented, would live and die without ever having left the slightest footprint on earth. Yes, they do have souls, made in the image of their Creator God, but no one seemed to care, not even me, as I whizzed passed them in my fancy car.

But some truly cared! The ones that Barbara and I were going to teach at the Rural Life Development Center—they cared. Those farmer-pastors and home-group leaders cared for these girls and the masses just like them. People with a caste or without a caste, the farmer-pastors only saw souls who needed Jesus. These valiant men and women came in droves to the Farm. They were taught how to make their own farms more profitable, as well as what the gospel is, and how it could be shared. In droves they spread all over the Khond Hills, improving lives of multiple thousands, and planting hundreds of house churches. They were taught by a lot of us, but it would be Calvin and Margaret Fox, guiding the powerful hands of Pastor Sudansu, who were used of God to alter an entire people group. The Kui people obtained a better life on earth. Masses of them were given the opportunity to receive Christ and have the hope of being with Him in heaven because of the Farm and these Giants who ministered through it.

We were glad when we arrived at the Farm and blessed to be a part of its effectiveness in God's kingdom.

BEING THERE

Normally, our trip to Raipada in the Khond Hills was a refreshing experience. The dorm rooms were comfortable enough in comparison to most other seminar places. The food was OK, but the fellowship with Calvin and Margaret was always exceptional. We knew the Foxes lived more simply than any other missionary couple we'd ever known. They were both farmers and their small block house reflected that fact. Every piece of furniture in the house was strictly utilitarian except for an older couch and one soft chair that had a pole lamp beside it. Their nightly entertainment was reading. All of us were challenged by the price they were willing to pay toward the cost of being a major cog in God's wheel to change an entire people group. Both Calvin and Margaret will need neck braces to hold up their crowns in heaven.

In our previous visits, it was normal that the electricity was often not functioning in the rural areas of India, so we anticipated sitting out in the yard looking into a black, velvety, starry sky. We had drunk coffee and watched the constellation of Orion chase the Bear across the entire sky. Orion seemed to pull a whole wagon full of stars after him. It never got old or boring. Never!

However this particular visit wasn't a normal time. It was Sunday, January 24, 1999. Leaving the apartment in Bangalore, while heading to the airport, we caught the first wave of the tragic news. Graham Staines, an Australian missionary, with his two sons, ten-year-old Philip and six-year-old Timothy, had been burned to death the previous night. They had been killed in Manoharpur, Orissa, not a hundred miles from where we were headed. We joined literally hundreds of millions of folks, in India alone, in surreal shock.

"It's impossible! It couldn't have happened," we all told ourselves. Such horrendous evil would not fit in our minds, no matter how we turned it. But it had happened! Graham had ministered to the extremely poor and the lepers in that region of Orissa for decades. His parents before him had started their ministry in that very place more than thirty years previously. On Saturday evening, January 23, Graham left his wife and daughters in one of their ministry sites and drove with his sons to another, not far away. The three Staines were sleeping in the back of their van when a mob of fifty Hindu fanatics burst upon them with machetes and axes in hand. They doused the Staines' van with gasoline and set it ablaze. Reportedly, this evil mob used bamboo poles to keep the doors shut so that no one could get out of the burning vehicle. Testimonies from the captured gang members recorded that Graham pleaded with his attackers to let his sons live, but was resolutely denied. By then the fire had eaten through the interior. Again, eyewitnesses reported that Graham placed his boys under his protective body and prayed. I don't know what Graham Staines spoke to his precious sons that night as the mob howled like wild animals, but I can imagine that he might have said, "Hold on tight, boys, for we are about to see Jesus. It will be over quickly and we'll hug Jesus together." They did just that as that's the way their bodies were positioned after the fire was extinguished.

Raw revulsion and guttural cries of protest broke out all over India. Indians of every stripe were horrified by this evil. For days, even weeks, we would have Indians—total strangers—come up to us, some with tears in their eyes, and express genuine remorse. Their words for such unthinkable actions were, "Evil, inhuman, un-Indian, Satanic."

"The blood of the martyrs is the seed of the church," stated by Tertullian in the second century proved to be true in the 20th century, too. In the district around Manoharpur, Orissa, the church exploded with growth following this horrific event. One Baptist church planter who attended the LEAD seminars stated, "I've never been so busy sharing the gospel with Hindus before this happened." He went on to report that everyone was keenly interested in what kind of faith, or belief, could produce a life like Graham and Gladys Staines. She went back, with her daughters, and continued their ministries in that area of Orissa. In 2005, India awarded her the Patma Shree, the fourth highest civilian honor for her work in Orissa. Then in 2016, Gladys Staines received the Mother Teresa Memorial International Award for Social Justice. But, according to her own words, her greatest reward is that, through the grace of God, she is certain that Graham, Philip, and Timothy are with Jesus in heaven, and she will join them soon.

It was a different, but exciting time, to be in Orissa the week after this heartrending tragedy took place. We all were shocked that such a horrible action could take place anywhere, especially right there in their backyard. It stirred in all of us a desire and commitment to be even more effective in sharing the gospel. Each of us came out of the Khond Hills more devoted to Jesus and more dedicated to seeing His work accomplished than ever before.

2

THE HIMALAYAN WALKER

We met Brother Ratna Rai in Itahari, which is in the flatlands of East Nepal. The young Nepali Baptist Convention requested LEAD to train a group of lay pastors and church leaders who lived "out on the terrai" (flatland) of eastern Nepal. This leadership seminar was also accessible to a few "mountain men" who were church planters in the upper eastern region of the Himalaya Mountains. Bai (Brother) Rai was one of them. He had walked three eight-hour days to get to the terrai where he then took a bus for another five hours in order to get to Itahari. Bai Rai had been invited to attend one of the first Bible-teaching LEAD seminars in order to become equipped to start churches in the upper regions where oxygen was rarer than it was in Itahari.

Our first personal meeting took place during a morning break in that first seminar. Rai sat on a rock, warming himself in the midmorning sunshine with his shoes off. I walked over and knelt beside him. Danial Subba, the local pastor of the Baptist church where we conducted the seminar, was a very good translator and introduced me to Bai Rai. One of Rai's feet was puffed and reddish from an infection. We talked about getting some medicine from a local shop. Brother Rai was so appreciative of the attention. He had learned a bit of English from the British in yesteryear and could communicate on a limited basis.

Seeing that Rai was definitely older (sixty-two at that time), I asked him, "Bai Rai, what are you doing here? Why aren't you home with grandkids sitting in your lap?"

He smiled and gave an answer that has forever embedded itself in my soul. "Brother Harry, if I don't go, they will never know." He went on to explain that his limited exposure to actual Bible study made it difficult for him to answer many questions from the Hindus that he was trying to win to Christ. Rai was excited because, after studying for only a couple of days at the seminar, he was certain that he could answer many of their questions. With an engaging smile, he went on to add, "Now that I know more…I go more."

Another older participant, Brother Dil, sat beside Ratna Rai on the thatched mat which covered the dirt floor of the Baptist church building. Brother Dil made Rai look like a teenager, as Dil was ninety-two years old. He heard the gospel late in life and responded to Christ after all of his children were grown and gone. Though he was basically uneducated, Dil insisted on all of his children "getting schooled." All had become successful professionals while Dil continued living near the poverty line in his old farmhouse. The frosty wind of the bitterly cold Nepali winter would blow through the roughhewn planks of the walls of his old house. He slept on some padded bed slats which did not quite qualify as a mattress. He often climbed the switchback trail that connected his village with the small town below where he bought his supplies. More importantly to him, Dil went up and down these switchbacks to attend church every Sunday where he worshipped his Lord Jesus.

Dil's family had been horrified when he became a Christian. They commanded their father to renounce that "foreign religion." They said, "Give up this Christ and we will insure that you live in comfort for the rest of your life."

"Impossible!" cried Dil without compromise. "My Lord did not live in comfort, so neither will I!"

Dil and Rai sat on that church floor for six-and-a-half hours a day during the seminar. Dil's strong voice was often heard, "Sir/Madam, what was that verse?" or "Where is that found in the Bible?" Others told us that on any given Sunday that same strong voice was often heard preaching about Christ somewhere in the small town below his roughhewn farmhouse.

Bai Rai continued coming to each of the LEAD seminars which occurred every six months, "To get more and more," as he put it. For three long days he trekked down the mountain, capped by a rough bus ride for another half-day. Then for six days, he sat and then slept on the matted floor coverings of the church. He ate out of an outside kitchen and dining area, used an outhouse and washed off in a nearby creek. At the end of the week, Rai got back on his feet and reversed his previous steps until he returned home with his more.

Bai Rai was led by the Holy Spirit to an unusual church planting strategy. When the conditions allowed, he made a seven-day, clockwise trek from his mountain village. Sometimes the scenery was spectacular. The snow-covered Himalayan peaks expressed their glory toward their Creator who was above the richest blue sky ever seen on earth. At other times, the bitter, frozen wind attacked anything that stood upright and expelled all hidden heat from every fiber in the body. Whether in slick rain or icy, blowing snow, Rai took the next step and then another until he arrived at his next destination. As he walked on, Rai often stopped by a community well to share a song or tell a Bible story to anyone who would listen. Toward the end of the day, he would do the same at the village where he hoped to spend the night. He also offered to go and pray for anyone sick in the village. As is customary in that part of the world, Rai was frequently invited to spend the night with one of the village families. He would repeat this experience for the next seven days and nights, arriving back home on the eighth day. After a few days of rest, Rai would repeat that seven-day trek. It did not take long before God began to work, and casual interest was expressed in Rai's Jesus. That interest became more intense among a few of the villagers, especially the ones with whom he spent nights. These families had a growing desire to know more about this Jesus who loved them so much. These families invited others to come and hear about Jesus when Rai passed through, which birthed embryonic churches scattered along that seven-day trek.

After almost one year of those seven-day treks, Rai started a fourteen-day trek counterclockwise from his village. He used the same gospel approach—he sang songs, told Bible stories, prayed for the sick, and asked people to make a clear choice to receive Christ as their Savior. God blessed again, and small groups of believers started meeting to sing songs, pray, and read portions of Scripture. Bai Rai slowly helped each group appoint a local leader, a shepherd, who would lead the meetings when Rai was not available to do so. Those meetings grew into New Testament churches which dotted the mountainside like flowers in springtime.

There was a cost. Opposition came in the form of some beatings. Others threw rocks at Rai as though he were a rabid dog, accompanied by some hateful names shouted at him by a few Hindu leaders. One of the strongest forces of opposition were the Maoists who tried to capture the small country of Nepal. None of these things caused Rai to stumble, or stopped him from taking the next step. The thing that slowed him down the most was his failing health. Having lived and worked in extreme conditions of the upper regions of the Himalayas, Rai began to pass out along the trails he walked. Local villagers often found him and nourished him back to health before he continued his trek. Even strangers found him and took him to the next village where Rai was always welcomed, even by non-Christians. He was beloved by most. In each case, word was sent back to his wife and family with assurances of his care.

Unlike you and me, Rai had no competent medical facility available to him halfway up one of the Himalayan peaks. He did what every giant of the faith has done—he took the next step toward sharing Jesus with those surrounding him that did not know the Savior. Rai, therefore, planted gospel seeds that grew into churches which, after a while, started other churches. These pinpricks of light were scattered all over the huge mountainside. Rai did all of this by taking the next step, and that is why I named this Giant, The Himalayan Walker.

GETTING THERE

Before going to Itahari, E. Nepal, we had to first fly into Kathmandu, the capital of Nepal. On our first trip to Nepal we flew from Bangkok, Thailand, to Kathmandu. After three hours in the air, ragged, white-crowned peaks suddenly appeared on the right side of the aircraft—the Himalayas in all their glory. Then suddenly, actually shockingly, the plane jerked left, and the nose of the plane dipped downward. An audible gasp was heard throughout the plane. Apparently this maneuver was necessary because it happened on each subsequent flight to Kathmandu, although we never got used to it.

Kathmandu was nestled up into the neck of a U-shaped ridge that made this approach well calculated. The city sits at four-thousand-feet above sea level and is horseshoed by the Nagarkot ridge that rises up to seven-thousand feet. From that ridge, God's white-tipped fingerprints form a semicircle around the city. These perennial snow-covered mountains all stretch upward to well over twenty-thousand feet in their continual praise of their Creator. From that ridge on a clear day, you could see the Annapurna's and Himalaya's majestic peaks. That panoramic view automatically bends the knee in the heart of every fragile human observer and makes them feel like newly born babes just escaping their mother's wombs. This world is so big and so ancient and we were excited to be in it.

Kathmandu is a perfect transit place where the ancient and the modern hold hands. In the greater Kathmandu vicinity you can step back into history 1,500 years. In that same place, you can eat hamburgers in neat cafés where cappuccino coffees are also served. It is always cold. We often stayed overnights with missionary colleagues who served in Kathmandu. The houses seemed to shiver each time we entered them. It was said that those houses were built to withstand summer heat. We were certain they accomplished that feat by maintaining icicles within their walls until summertime. Brrr! In the evening hours all of us would sit around the living room, Nepali style, on the floor, propped up with large pillows. It was the only room in the entire house that had a heater in it. Though we only went in the spring and fall, never in dead of winter, it still was teeth-chattering cold. Of course we would have our coats on even in that "warm" room. But when we left the warmth of that room to go to the bedroom, a chill sliced through every fiber of our bodies. It made for very, very quick baths, followed by a leap into the bed under a thick duck-down comforter. We learned quickly not to move out of our body-shaped warmed spot on the bed, as it felt as if frozen ice picks stabbed us each time we did.

Mornings could not come fast enough where hot coffee was available. The only thing better than that cup of hot coffee was the warm fellowship extended to us by those gracious hosts. We treasured those satisfying times.

First we conducted a LEAD seminar in West Nepal, either in Kathmandu or Pokhara where Mt. Machapuchare (Fish-Tail) was always visible. Because this mountain is believed to be connected to the Hindu god of Shiva, it is never allowed to be climbed. From W. Nepal we flew to E. Nepal for the second Nepali seminar. The small eighteen-passenger prop plane could barely clear the seven-thousand-foot hills that almost surrounded Kathmandu. We flew so close to the top of those ridges that I had the urge to lift my feet, and expected to see tree limbs in the wheel struts when we landed. We felt like we could have shaken hands with the people on the ground as we flew over their neighborhoods. The land swooped up like a gigantic wave so we saw minute details, like partially painted window frames in some of the houses. Then the land sloped away into darkened valleys, so far downward it literally took our breaths away. After about one-and-a-half hours, we landed on a narrow, potholed airstrip in the metropolis of Biratnagar, E. Nepal. They brought out metal steps without handrails so that we could exit the plane. The faded paint on the terminal building reminded me of some older barns I'd seen on the backroads of North Carolina, and the upkeep was about the same.

Bruce Burk, a Baptist missionary and one of the most valuable assets that the LEAD ministry had anywhere, lived in Dharan, E. Nepal. He arranged for all of our East Nepal seminars. He transported us from Biratnagar to Itahari, which took about forty-five minutes in "Bruce-time," not a regular driver's time. Being with Bruce was like downing a large, double-strength energy drink. Bruce's spirit, sparked by his vision, recharged ours every time. He had walked with, and beside, many of the men who came to that seminar, and was so excited about the difference LEAD made in his Giants. We were as well.

BEING THERE

Itahari was just a village that grew out of its pants into town status. The Hotel Aangan was a total misnomer. Hotel, it was not! Aangan was like a village lodge pressed into a hotel's function. It was noisy, dirty, and understaffed, with only one English speaker who stayed at the desk. Bruce always got us the best room, which was on the second floor. It cost us $8.50 and was worth every cent. We climbed the stairs with luggage in hand, passed the walls that had a light coat of paint overlaid with a heavy coat of dirt. On each landing the walls sported red splotches of betel-nut spit (like chewing tobacco). Actually, the spit added decoration to a very drab interior. We remembered the bed as one you did not fall back onto. It was basically covered planks on which you eased onto and off. The pillows would have been handy on any fishing boat where an extra anchor might be needed. Surprisingly, the bathroom had a Western-style commode, without a seat, of course. We sat on the porcelain rim. They even provided toilet paper daily, if it was requested. We noticed that toilet paper rolls were the skinniest we'd ever seen. It dawned on us that some proprietor was removing the wrapper and reducing the sheets by half. Of course, the price remained the same. However, the hotel did provide hot water, even though it was a struggle. The hot water arrived only after we walked down to the kitchen and requested it. A while later, a boy struggled to bring a bucket of slimy, warm water to our door. At times there were still vegetable parts or leaves on top of the water. We finally surmised that they were heating our bath water in the same pot in which they cooked some of their vegetables, hence, the grease and floating leaves. It worked out just fine as we didn't squeak much as we walked back and forth from the church.

In spite of some of these inconveniences, we taught God's Word to some of the most spiritually needy pastors and church planters anywhere in Asia. A few of these men and women were semiliterate. Many had only recently obtained a complete Bible in their own ethnic language and had not yet read it through completely. However, because they were called by God to be Shepherds, they devoted themselves totally to leading their groups or churches. Often, at night, a large group of these participants met together in the church building and did their homework together. More often than not they discovered more truth during those times than during the teaching sessions in the day time. On the following days, after a fruitful evening of learning, they beamed with joy after being able to answer one of our questions. They had grasped a biblical truth or understood one of God's promises and were overjoyed with it. Those were precious times of great reward for us. We saw some who were starved for His nourishment and then heard their joyous exclamations when filled by His Word. This made our cups of joy brim over. It also made the sore backs, slick baths, and cold nights absolutely worth being there. These were God's Giants in the making. They came in various packages: old, inexperienced, women in a man's world, handicapped, and uneducated. Most all were poor, and yet they had been Spirit-picked to be fruitful in each place in which they served. They only needed adequate feeding. Barbara and I had that fantastic privilege and responsibility. We lived with that joyous burden day in and night out. We knew that when we gave more, they would know more, and like the Himalayan Walker, would go more. And God smiled more.

3

The Heart and Tongue of An Evangel

Naveed's presence demanded attention. He was a daunting Evangel with alert eyes that penetrated our souls. He immediately became embedded in our hearts, never to be dislodged. He was the primary translator for our LEAD seminars in both Karachi and Jhelum, Pakistan. He not only translated our words, but our hearts also. His gifts were innumerable.

A reverse gear had not been installed in his spiritual motor, as was seen by words written in English and Urdu on his small van, "Jesus loves you." This van was not driven in Birmingham, Alabama, or Macon, Georgia, but in Karachi, Pakistan, and throughout that rugged land.

This Evangel was converted out of a staunch Muslim family. Like Saul of Tarsus in the New Testament, once he was convinced Jesus was the Savior for the whole world, he took up his cross and followed Jesus. Since then, Naveed has preached continuously on Christian radio stations, and was even on national TV during one of the Christmas celebrations. He has also created an evangelical organization, The New Life Institute, through which he has published a copious amount of printed and digital materials.

Hundreds, maybe even thousands, have found Christ through his ministries, but one of the most impressive ministries is Naveed's Friday

Seeker's Class. He conducts this service in his own apartment where he lives with his wife and two children. It is a modest two-bedroom apartment in which they converted its largest room into a study. Naveed teaches discipleship studies to church members there. He also has special studies for believers who have not yet openly declared their faith in Jesus. This study is usually done before their baptism service. Baptisms often are followed by severe persecution, including death threats and attempts thereof. Therefore, Naveed feeds their souls to prepare for such reality so that these babes in Christ will be ready for this predictable persecution before it happens. Such is the price of the ticket for a Muslim in Pakistan to receive Christ and identify openly with his or her Savior.

Naveed himself had been beaten seven times for his decision to follow Christ. His name appeared often on a hit list published in Karachi. He said, "I don't plan on being an old man," indicating his willingness to die for Christ. But Naveed's greatest concern was that someone may roll a couple of hand grenades into his apartment, killing or maiming those most precious to him on earth, his wife and two children. He lived with that burden, day after day, throughout the years.

One day my travel schedule allowed me to be in Karachi on a Friday. Naveed invited me to attend the Seeker's meeting. The room was large. It hosted an intricately patterned Persian rug that covered most of the floor space. There were fifteen men, all sitting or kneeling on the rug, facing Naveed. In accordance with their cultural practice, each was barefooted, having left their shoes or sandals at the door. Each participant had a butterfly-shaped book holder sitting in front of him supporting a copy of the Bible in Urdu, the official language of Pakistan. Naveed and a few others also had copies of the Koran in front of them so that they could compare the teachings about Isa from the Koran with the teachings about Jesus from the Bible. Islam teaches that it is a serious offense to put the Koran on the floor, as that is their holy book.

Pakistani Christians have adopted the same position for their holy book, the Bible. Naveed's class coincided with the hour that Muslims went to their mosques on Friday so that the seekers would not be obvious. Some dressed in white punjabis, with waistcoats and a turban. Others wore regular punjabis with black peci hats, oval-shaped Muslim caps. A few had white skullcaps, indicating they had made the pilgrimage to Mecca, fulfilling one of the five pillars of Islam. This was a serious group.

After an hour-and-a-half of animated discussion and Naveed sharing from both holy books, he invited his preteen daughter to read a portion of Scripture and pray. Naveed kneeled behind his daughter, casting his shadow over her. Then he concluded the service with a benediction.

Neelam, Naveed's daughter, read from Matthew. I could not understand a word but in that moment, God came down and visited that room. She had the perfect blend of deep confidence, absent of any arrogance. She exuded humility before her God and her guests. When Neelam prayed, I had to peek because I truly expected to see Jesus standing there in the room with His pierced hands spread wide. I've rarely, if ever, been on a higher spiritual peak or bathed in a more intimate spiritual embrace with Almighty God as on that Friday afternoon in Karachi, Pakistan. I know I'll meet some who attended that session when I get to heaven; I just know it.

Another special moment with this daunting Evangel occurred at Marge Worten's final teaching session in Karachi. The Wortens were retiring from LEAD, and that session was the last time they would teach this group of Karachi pastors. Naveed had explained to me what had happened when Von and Marge Worten taught the first LEAD seminar in Karachi, about eleven years earlier. As Marge approached the podium in that first seminar, Pastor Stephen, who was one of the senior pastors in the group, stood and spoke frankly against a woman teaching men.

It just wasn't done in Pakistan. He was not rude but adamant. Naveed had to explain to the group that all LEAD teams were comprised of couples and if they would not allow women to teach, then LEAD could not minister to them in Karachi. At that time, Naveed and the Wortens negotiated a trial week of LEAD teaching. Afterwards, a decision would be made concerning future LEAD seminars in Karachi. At the end of that first seminar, Pastor Stephen stood again and said that God had used "Sister Marge" to marvelously teach God's Word, and asked if they would continue to come and send other LEAD teams to Karachi. That was a near miracle.

Now, at the end of Marge's final teaching session in Karachi before retiring, all the participants rose to their feet and praised God vocally. Pastor Stephen, older and slower now, made his way to the front. Naveed translated his heartfelt appreciation for "my sister Marge." Then something happened that caused time to stand still. In a land where a man never touches a woman who is not of his own family, Pastor Stephen reached out and placed his right hand on Marge's forehead and pronounced a blessing that was usually used for a departing wife or daughter. Clearly Pastor Stephen was stating that he not only accepted Marge as a teacher but also as a beloved adopted daughter. Truly it was a precious moment and made even tenderer as Naveed communicated "heart-words" and blended two distinct worlds into one koinonia heartbeat.

Without a doubt, Naveed was the daunting Evangel of Pakistan. He could blend worlds into one understandable unit through his ability to translate, not only what the mouth said, but what the heart shared. With his soul-penetrating eyes, brilliant smile, and lack of reverse in his spiritual gearbox, he was used by God to draw a multitude of Pakistanis into God's kingdom.

GETTING THERE

We always flew P.I.A. (Pakistan International Airlines) domestically and it was an adventure every time. The P.I.A. pilots were all former Pakistani Air Force pilots and many of them, obviously, were former fighter pilots. In fact, the locals said that P.I.A. stood for "Please Inform Allah," because arriving at one's destination was always in doubt. On one trip in March of 1996, we had one of those adventures.

"Pakistan International Airlines Flight 300 Crashes: All lost including three Baptist missionary couples"—This could have been a small article on page four in the local paper on March 18, 1996. The Wortens, Napiers, and Bushes all boarded P.I.A. flight 300 from Karachi to the capital city of Islamabad. The weather was not bad but began to deteriorate as we reached 27,000 feet. We could hear distant peals of thunder and see flicks of lightning far away on the horizon. The seatbelt sign flashed on. Suddenly, it seemed as if we had run off of a silky smooth interstate highway onto a washboard, rutted country road at interstate speeds. The plane started shuddering and bouncing as though it were making a water landing in turbulent seas. Barbara and I grasped hands and looked out of the side portals. Thunder pounded like a kettle drummer gone mad. Lightning streaked and splintered through the rain-soaked skies. The wings seemed to flap like an old gooney bird caught in a storm. The plane soared upwards one minute and plummeted downward the next. Then it happened! The nose of the 747 dove straight downward. We were hurtling toward the rugged, rocky terrain at 644 mph, according to the wall monitor. Barbara and I squeezed hands. I looked across the aisle at Von and Marge. They, too, were clasping hands. Von gave me a slight nod, to which I responded likewise. We were going down. We would be greeting Jesus in just a minute or two. Then, just as suddenly as when we had started the dive, we leveled off a couple thousand feet above the ground into perfectly

calm air. There were numerous shouts of "Allah!" with some exclamations of "Praise God!" and a few who said "Thank you, Jesus." All in a
day's work for the fighter pilot who had gotten us safely through, or
better, under the storm. Therefore we had the opportunity to prepare
for another seminar. As we deplaned, I noticed more than one person
who kneeled and kissed the ground. Barbara and I, still holding hands,
looked up and again thanked our Lord and Protector.

BEING THERE

The LEAD seminars in Karachi were all conducted at a Catholic
retreat center named The Monastery of Angels. It sat nestled on the
edge of the huge megalopolis of Karachi. The center was an excellent
facility, providing well-equipped classrooms, tasty food and a peaceful
environment. One reason for the peaceful atmosphere was that all the
nuns who inhabited the monastery lived under a vow of silence. They
spoke not a word, nor did they care to hear one. This situation presented
challenges when adjustments or repairs were needed. Basically, those
were accomplished through written notes left in the dining hall. Dining
room doors remained closed except when it was time to eat. At such
times, the doors would discreetly be opened when the food was on the
table ready to eat. We never saw nor spoke to any of them, only passed
notes when necessary.

The gardens were a feast for the eyes. Flowering bushes spotted
the area like early drops of rain preceding a summer squall. They were
exclamation points of beauty. Plots of multicolored flowers sprung forth
around trees, sidewalks, and along the ten-foot-high wall surrounding
the compound. Webs of sidewalks stretched out over the gardens
enticing participants to take walks in late afternoons before supper was
served.

It was during this period of dusk when we experienced a

phenomenon that never occurred outside of that garden. An apparition appeared above a large evergreen bush. The bush was twelve-feet-tall and about fifteen-feet-wide. Two to three feet above the bush there appeared to be a dancing gaseous bubble. That form extended another six to eight feet upward and about four feet sideways. The problem was that the undulating cloud was shape-shifting. In one moment it looked like a cone, then a coke bottle, then a figure skater, never settling on one form. It was like a buzzing liquid cloud. Suddenly at that point, we realized the cloud was a swarm of mosquitoes, thousands upon thousands of them. They buzzed through various shapes for about five minutes and then dissipated, only to return again a few minutes later. How and why? Only their Creator could answer that question. Every evening, we were mesmerized by this sight.

The Monastery of the Angels hosted a great facility with one exception: their guest bedrooms. We wondered if some unrepentant, demon-possessed monk might have designed the twin beds in each room. Each bed felt like miniature railroad rails had been placed in each bed at devious angles. The body could not be contorted in such a way to miss these demonic works. Sleep was punctuated throughout the night with being awakened by painful bones that stretched over the tracks. Raked shoulders, crushed backbones, or banged hipbones loudly complained each evening. The ongoing question was how did this demonic design get applied to each and every bed in the guest rooms? We tried them all.

One night, I'd had my quota of suffering, so I pulled the paper-thin mattress off the bed and placed it on the floor. We had to use burning mosquito coils every night (and in all other places that LEAD taught) to keep the buzz bombers off of us. I had to move it farther away. With my posterior end and shoulder lying squarely on the concrete floor, but no railroad rail, I had almost drifted back to sleep when I felt something scurry across my bare leg. Yes, it was hot in those rooms. A quick spot with my flashlight revealed a host of tiny creatures, some known, others yet to be named. Among them were a couple of the largest roaches I'd ever seen. Their front feelers seemed as long as radio antennas. Unnerved as I was, the "railroad bed" still had me debating until I saw two beady red dots staring at me, belonging to one of the largest rats I'd ever seen inside a building. Then it was four little reddish eyes and I suddenly realized it wasn't the roaches that tracked across my legs. With the debate over, I reluctantly returned to the higher regions of my comfortless bed. I returned the burning coil back between our two beds, hoping for protection, not only from the aerial attacks but also from the floor warfare too.

We have been asked why we would put up with beady eyes and torturous rails in our beds each time we came to the Monastery of the Angels. The answer was simple: Not only was God teaching us patience and priorities, but He continued to use us as His chisels and sandpaper to shape these pastors and church leaders in Karachi. He used us both directly, and indirectly. Directly, we taught God's Word in a down-to-earth manner that they could understand and imitate. Indirectly, we interacted with them during meals and the break periods, sharing our hearts, experiences, and vision with them.

On one occasion, a pastor asked me if my own father had loved me. He wanted to know if my father had ever embraced or hugged me; if he had ever said, "I love you, son." When I answered yes, he just drooped his head. This pastor had never heard one affirmative word from his father, nor ever had he been embraced by him. He said that the men LEAD teachers had helped him to visualize a loving Heavenly Father.

We also often heard comments about how LEAD's teachers had helped their marriages. By observing how we lovingly interacted with our mates and showed mutual respect to each other, they went home with a commitment to do the same. We had not only taught them truths from God's Word but we had incarnated it before them.

Results in Karachi? Churches grew larger. Home fires burned brighter and warmer. God had done this through a group of teachers, who remained faithful to live out His Word as well as to teach it effectively. Therefore, a few rickety rail beds, creepy crawlers, or even beady eyes would not alter our commitment and privilege to be with our brothers and sisters in Karachi.

4

A SMALL MAN
WITH A BIG HEART

Pastor Veerna, all of five-feet, six-inches tall and weighing maybe one-hundred-thirty pounds, could not be stopped nor deterred from serving "the livin' Got (God)," as Veerna pronounced. Veerna lived in the heartland of India in a village so remote that it wasn't even on the Indian maps. He lived in Parlakhemundi, Andhra Pradesh, Central India.

We taught Christian leadership materials based on Scripture to both men and women. It was the only formal teaching that the majority of these participants experienced. Barbara and I adapted the written materials to form an amalgamation of Sunday school lessons, basic theological truths, and a smattering of seminary-level instructions. Pastor Veerna always sat on the front row with a chair turned backwards so he could use it like a desk. He always had two or three men with him that he was grooming to be church leaders and maybe even pastors. Taking notes, Pastor Veerna constantly pled in a soft whispering voice, "Slowly, Mr. Harry, slowly; for I must get everything you say."

The issue was that Veerna had some restrictions which for a lesser man would be extreme handicaps. For one, he had Coke-bottle glasses so thick that they seemed to weigh down his whole head. Then, each lens was cracked in diagonal degrees which created a V-shape. I can't imagine how he focused with them. Without them, he could not see ten feet away nor read the largest print. Another challenge he faced was that his left arm was a nub just below the elbow. Word had it that Veerna lost his left arm trying to scare off, or kill off, the wild boars that kept crashing through the bamboo fence around his little garden. The practice was to place something akin to a cherry bomb down in the furrows of his garden to ward off the wild boars. Unfortunately, Veerna was too close when one of them exploded. He lost most of his left forearm and had some internal damage. He survived it with "Got's grace and mercy." On two other occasions, wild elephants charged through the bamboo wall surrounding the little housing area where he lived and literally tore down every house. Veerna got his family to safety and then went back with torches to encourage the huge beasts to go back from where they had come. One thing this five-feet, six-inch, one-hundred-thirty-pound man, with a nub for an arm, did not lack was courage. He backed down from nothing! Oh, he could make wise tactical retreats, but he would never surrender.

Pastor Veerna was the pastor of a Baptist church not far from Parlakhemundi. Its building consisted of six stout poles with a leafy thatched bamboo roof. It had a dirt floor and a few handmade, backless, wooden benches. Also, the church had a man of God; a man without many peers who loved them and shepherded them like few others could do. He also fearlessly preached God's Word to them every week.

Because Pastor Veerna had become "handicapped" through an accident, he had a heart for those born that way. He and his wonderful wife were mostly responsible for the rescue and call into the ministry of Anand Kumar.

Anand was born in a poor village just outside of Parlakhemundi. To be different in Anand's world was synonymous with being ridiculed. After all, if the gods laughed at you, why shouldn't everyone else? To be physically or mentally handicapped, or deformed, while living in staunch poverty anywhere in the developing world, like in Parlakhemundi, tattooed a person as one cursed. This handicap inflicted a life of living agony on such a person. Anand was such a person. Many parents, in these circumstances, killed their "not-normal" offspring. Also, unfortunately, many of the handicapped who survived ended their own lives because of the suffocating hopelessness and the constant searing of their souls from those who mocked and ridiculed them.

Anand experienced all of these challenges because his eyes could not focus, and instead wandered from side to side. He was thought to be an "idiot"; hence, he was offered no schooling. Since his mother and father barely eked out a living through subsistence farming, there was no money for soap or toothpaste, and such for a "cursed one." So as an older child, Anand was snaggle-toothed and had acne pox marks. It was a lot easier to pull rotten teeth than to fix them, especially for one of "them."

However, the gospel is blind to outward imperfections. Anand heard the gospel while he sat by one of those six poles in Pastor Veerna's village church. He worked at memorizing the gospel songs when Veerna's wife became aware of him. She showed Anand agape love and, with heavenly patience, began to repair one of God's creations. Veerna got Anand into a Christian orphanage where transformation occurred. It was startling. Anand had a bright mind and could do mathematics far beyond his age group. But his heart was set on serving the Lord, like Veerna and his wife who had become his heart-adopted "Mama and Daddy."

After high school, and then Bible school, Anand returned to assist Pastor Veerna in his ministry. At the time we began teaching in Parlakhemundi, Anand had married and had two small daughters. After learning that God wanted churches to start more churches, Pastor Veerna, Anand, and two or three trainees started three more churches. Veerna gave one-half of his twenty-five-dollar monthly salary in order to buy materials to build other church buildings.

When I asked Pastor Veerna how he could do that, his simple response was, "How could I not? The Got told me to do it, so I do it!" This small man cast a shadow far over my head and his huge heart challenged mine to be more like him and "his Got."

GETTING THERE

Getting to Parlakhemundi takes rank determination. Drivers had to know where it was before they left Hyderabad or they would never find it. It is a seven-plus-hour car trip. We passed through farmland where laborers barely eked out an existence, interspersed with wasteland between the small farming communities. On one such trip I counted seventeen overturned or burned-out vehicles that were still in the road from recent accidents. One of these was a tanker truck. It was burnt beyond description. There was nothing left to scavenge; even the tires had become ashes. The truck had hit a bridge embankment running at highway speeds of probably 45 mph. Another of the seventeen wrecks was a bus on one side of the road in front of a one-way bridge with a large truck on the other side of the road; both going the same direction. The bus was in an L shape, wrapped around the embankment on the left side. The truck was smashed into the embankment on the right side. The cab was obliterated. It looked like a giant hand had pancaked it into the cargo section behind the cab. These two vehicles were going much faster than any reasonable nighttime highway speeds. Apparently, the two drivers were racing with each other to get to the one-way bridge first and neither of them would back down. As usual with these road accidents, the vehicles had been stripped like piranhas strip a cow that wanders into its waters. Seemingly both accidents were weeks old, not hours. These sights always reminded us that life was precarious on these two-lane highways.

One of the factors causing this kind of accident at night was that the drivers often depend on stimulants to get them through the long nights. Of course that situation is not limited to India, by any means. Everything is used, such as alcohol and barbiturates. It is not unusual that those drivers worked a daytime job and drove all night, as well. Life in India forces people to push themselves beyond human limits. The metal skeletons strewn along side of the highways of India attest to that fact.

You really had to want, or need, to get to Parlakhemundi to make this trip. The heat ravages you. The pavement literally simmers with heat waves. Dust and grit blast you through the open windows of the car making you feel like you are in an automatic sand blaster. An open car window is the only hope of surviving a long and trying trip. It doesn't take long to have owl-like white rings around your eyes outlining where your sunglasses protected not only your eyes, but the tender skin around them.

Many times we slowed to a crawl and gingerly bumped our way through herds of cattle leisurely wandering down the paved road. I asked our very patient driver what would happen if he plowed into such a herd and killed some of the cattle. He just shuddered. Then he shared that if a driver hits and kills a human being walking in the road, the normal prison sentence was about seven years. But if a driver hit and killed a cow, and he managed to survive the locals who would drag him out of the car and bludgeon him, then his court sentence would be life in prison. It occurred to me that Hindus believe the cow is sacred and therefore the cow's life is vastly more important than that of any mere human being. I suddenly realized why our driver was so patient as he eased through the herds of cattle in the middle of the road.

There are always challenges in getting to Parlakhemundi. Anytime you are on Indian highways for more than seven hours, you endure both physical and emotional trials. But getting to Parlakhemundi was worth it because it gave us the opportunity to teach men like Pastor Veerna, and twenty-nine more like him.

BEING THERE

We loved teaching in Parlakhemundi, not necessarily being there. This small Central Indian town was not a metropolis. Nestled down in an extensive farming area, goods and services were at a minimum. However, they had a two-story lodge (not a hotel) that catered to travelling Indian businessmen. The upkeep, sanitary conditions and maintenance, all reflected that reality.

Our first trip to Parlakhemundi was a memory-maker. We arrived shortly after dark. The LEAD coordinator for the area had reserved the best room in the lodge (and it was). This room, however, was on the second floor. After getting all our belongings into the room, everyone left to prepare for the start of the seminar on the next day. After an arduous seven-hour, sizzling car ride, we were beat. There was one fifteen-watt lightbulb hanging down on a wire from the ceiling. The ceiling was off-grey in color, the walls needed more paint, and the floors were grimy. Dead flying varmints were scattered across the dirty sheet on the bed. There was no cover sheet. In the LEAD ministry, we had learned to carry items like a couple of hundred-watt bulbs, a cover sheet, drop cords, mosquito coils, and a host of other things needed to make living spaces more tolerable.

I changed the bulb, ours for theirs, and—voila—the ceiling had not been painted grey but was totally entombed in cobwebs. It was a spider's heavenly kingdom. Barbara served as a summer missionary to the Seminole Indians in the Florida Everglades during her college days where she learned to put up with roaches, leeches, snakes, and even alligators, but the daddy longlegs spiders almost finished her off. There was no way Barbara was going to spend a night in that room as it was. Then we discovered the bathroom. Yuk! It had the usual squatty potty, which was a cement slab with a hole in the middle and two slightly raised places for the feet on each side of the hole. Clearly the users, in the past ten years, had either been drunk or had terrible aim when using this facility. The caked brown and black "lava flow" smeared the entire cement facility and had poured out onto the bathroom floor. Also the walls had been used as "target practice" for the betel-nut chewers, as there were multiple reddish splotches on all four walls. In addition to those things, there was a tiny corner sink which had black and grey grime all over it. But the most unusual aspect to this sink was that it had a hose in the place of the drain pipe. But the hose only extended three-fourths of the way to the floor. Therefore every time you used the sink, you washed your hands and your feet at the same time.

Dead tired or not, we needed to clean the place before getting started on the preparations for teaching at eight o'clock the next morning. I ran downstairs, across the dirt street and bought some cleansing materials and brushes. I grabbed a broom from the hotel and charged back upstairs. Barbara started in the bathroom while I removed the cobweb kingdom with a broom. We cleaned, swept, sprayed, and rubbed some more. We put our sheet on the bottom and turned theirs upside down and placed it on top. With the hundred-watt bulb we saw all we needed to see and cleaned it all. Then we heard some "tee hee-hee" giggles. We had not noticed, but there was a hole in the wall where an AC unit had been removed or never installed. Some kids were delighted with their free night of entertainment until I shooed them away and put a large cloth over the hole. By that time, I had added an extra mosquito coil that kept the buzz bombers at bay. The ancient fan was groaning but turned adequately. We were beyond exhaustion. The pipe coming out of the wall in the bathroom, that had once had a shower head attached but no longer did, produced an adequate stream of cold water for our baths. We bathed and crashed into the hard, lumpy bed but had no trouble sleeping that night.

We had time to review the following day as morning came early in Parlakhemundi. Believe it or not, we were excited to be there, in spite of all of the challenges. We were truly excited because there were thirty men and women, God's choice servants, who came with hopes of growing spiritually into better, more fully equipped men and women of God. They would be stretched upward toward their potential by the end of the week's teaching. That's what LEAD did! And we were privileged to be a part of that process in Parlakhemundi that week.

5

A Burmese Giant
in the Teakwood Forest

It was a hot, sweltering jungle afternoon in a refugee camp in northern Thailand. The camp was just across the Moei River separating Burma (Myanmar) from Thailand. A Giant of a man was being honored with the conferring of an Honorary Doctorate degree, presented by the Asian Baptist Graduate Theological Seminary located in Baggio, Philippines. And guess what? CNN was not there!

Saw Simon only stood a tall five-feet, four-inches, but cast a gigantic shadow over twenty-five thousand Burmese refugees in the Mae La valley. He was tenderly honored with the title of Thra Simon ("Teacher" Simon). This title clearly connected him to another historic Man who probably was not much taller, to whom His disciples often referred as "Teacher." Both Jesus and Simon were men of unalterable commitment, which led One to a cross and the other to a harsh jungle existence. As a teacher, one of Simon's life goals was to obtain his doctorate. It took a Giant the size of Thra Simon to draw people from America and the Philippines to this jungle spot in order to confer that degree upon one so deserving.

In his earlier life, Saw Simon lived comfortably in Rangoon, Burma (now Yangon, Myanmar), where he taught in a Baptist seminary. He had risen through the conventional levels of academia, earning a Master of Theology. Then Simon got an opportunity to attend the ABGTS in the Philippines to work on his doctorate. He finished his coursework and returned to Myanmar to write his dissertation. Not long after returning home, Thra Simon found himself running through the jungles of western Burma, a step ahead of attacking soldiers of the military Junta which had seized the government in a coup. The Karen People, Simon's people group, were the only Christian group among the eight larger ethnic tribes in Burma. They were being attacked by the ardent Buddhist-based military junta. Blood had been spilt all along the trail as they fled from their tribal land to the Moei River.

Thousands of Karen crossed the river into northern Thailand. At that point, the Karen became "a stateless people." Simon's people were not afforded refugee status. They were not given temporary Thai status. They were kept in harsh camps with restricted travel abilities. They could not work in local industries or in agriculture. They had to build their own houses and plant crops to provide enough food to meet their most basic needs. They were in a desperate, life-challenging predicament. Thra Simon was among the thousands, carrying his own precious babies in his arms across the Moei River to escape the massacre. Instead of drooping his head and crying in the mud, he lifted his head, and seized the opportunity to teach a whole new generation how to live for God and serve Him, in spite of the difficulties.

Thra Simon immediately became the principal of the Kawthooli Karen Baptist Bible School. This school primarily prepared leadership to return to Burma to evangelize the entire country. In the following seven to eight years, the KKBTS would graduate 168 graduates from its four-year program of study and place each one of these graduates in a ministry position in one of the many refugee camps in the Mae La Valley. Only a man of vision, a man of commitment, a genuine man of God who was truly a giant among men, could have produced such results. He set the vision. He set the standard. He forged more than survival. He forged victory day after day, night after mosquito-bitten night. Thra Simon made a heavenly contribution in a hellish reality.

After the appropriate speeches and most solemn ceremony, the Hooding of Thra Simon took place. Two American missionaries, both having earned doctorate degrees themselves, joined Dr. Graham Walker from the ABGTS and slipped the stole around Simon's neck and placed the mortarboard on his head. A roar erupted from the crowd of two-thousand-strong sitting in the handcrafted tabernacle. The thatched bamboo walls vibrated, and the teak-leaf roof rose with the continuous and thunderous applause. Though they were in a monsoon-like rain, a mass of people barely scratching out an existence saw one of their own smash a hole in one of the black container walls of depression that surrounded them, allowing a brilliant flash of hope to come pouring through.

Dr. Saw Simon slowly moved to the podium. The place became instantly quiet. Simon gazed out among the mass of Karen refugees, gave a polite nod of honor to his people, and simply stated, "I thank God for this honor. I receive it as a gift for our people." He bowed his head again to those thousands of Karen in front of him, giving them his sincere respect and honor and quickly returned to his seat. At five-feet, four-inches tall, fewer men have ever stood taller or cast a larger shadow than Thra Simon. CNN missed it, but I am glad that I was present to see the honoring of this Giant.

GETTING THERE

In the early days, getting to the Mae La camp required a trip to and through Bangkok, Thailand. Bangkok always smelled crowded. The air hung like a dirty sheet, never flapping, always hot and sizzling, or wet and sultry.

Moving through Bangkok or getting out of it was always nerve-wracking. The city had wasted money on the painted lane lines on the roads because they were ignored by all. Motorists pressed from curb to curb a glob across the three to four "planned lanes." There were cars, busses, large and small delivery trucks, a myriad of motorbikes, scooters, and cycles with innumerable bicycles filling up every crack of space on every street. Added to the mix, swarms of people walked with and through traffic. At peak hours we measured progress by centimeters, certainly not kilometers. There were times when we got off of the bus or out of the taxi and walked the last ten or fifteen blocks to our destination. We would always beat the vehicular travel because of the jams.

Once out of Bangkok, the road conditions changed drastically for the better. The British had helped Thailand build an excellent highway system similar to our interstates. Included in them were rest stops with decent restroom facilities. But that's where the Western bubble got popped. Guys took care of business in a long trough with no side privacy boards, while a cleaning lady mopped the floor and sang in a sing-song voice behind them. Unnerved did not come close to the feeling every time.

Our mission organization secured a vehicle for us to drive to Mae Sot, a border town with a bridge across the Moei River into Myanmar. It was the closest town to the Mae La Valley where the Baptist school was located. Getting to the camp from Mae Sot required another one-and-a-half hours of travel. These roads were quite different from the highway system. They were two-lane county roads, paved from one side to almost the other side. A sizable truck could have been lost in some of their potholes. Also, there were no signposts anywhere. Adding to the challenge was finding the correct dirt road off one of these country roads that led to the Kawthooli Karen Baptist Bible School in the Mae

La camp. We needed to be part treasure hunter and part bloodhound to find the correct two-lane trail to the school's location.

Another shock that jolted us was when the military stopped us at various check points. This was a frontier outpost far from downtown Bangkok. They spoke little English and we spoke no conversational Thai. We had no official paperwork other than our visas. We were just tourists who wanted to help some of the poor stateless peoples in the camps. The one factor that always helped was to try to communicate that we were teachers. The general Thai population reveres teachers to such an extent that once we communicated we were teachers, the soldiers became far more agreeable. Still, they examined the vehicle thoroughly. Every time this happened, we were grateful to God that we were under His protective umbrella. But it also scored our hearts to know the desperate conditions that our Karen brothers and sisters lived under minute by minute, 24/7. They were not even refugees, which would have placed them under the United Nations' supervision. They were "stateless." Being stateless meant they had no national or local authority to which to appeal when wrongs were done to them. Nightmarish wrongs were done to them often; so very often. The Karen People truly are remarkable people.

BEING THERE

Being with the Karen People in the Mae La camp required a different kind of setup than in most of the other places where we "walked with Giants." For reasons of safety and our health, we could not stay in the Mae La camp where the school was located. Malaria was endemic there. Each week we taught at the school, two-to-five students would come down with malaria and would have to miss some of the lessons. Since our schedule was filled up for the following two to three months, we could not afford that exposure of contracting malaria. So we stayed at the Porn Thet Hotel in Mae Sot, which was ninety minutes away from the camp. We travelled back and forth every day for five days. We never gave the name of our hotel to any of our American constituency, as the meaning of "porn" in the Thai language is quite different than it is in English. This hotel was one of the best we experienced anywhere on our teaching trek. It had electricity, hot water, and AC and sometimes they all functioned at the same time. This made it unlike most other places we stayed.

While in Mae Sot, a visit to the Lotus Flower restaurant was required. It was owned by a Texan and his Thai wife. Some of the Western dishes were recognizable, but what was essential, especially toward the end of the week, was one of their milkshakes. They truly were unbelievable. Those shakes were so thick that if you knocked one over, I don't believe much would spill. The Lotus Flower was one of God's serendipities for us. I imagined God giving us a wink and smile each time we savored one of those shakes in Mae Sot, Thailand.

Another factor in ministering in the KKBTS was that the camp, including the school, functioned according to the Myanmar time zone even though located in Thailand. This decision served to remind each person that one day they would return home. It contributed hope to a people in a desperate situation. The time difference between Mae Sot, Thailand, and the Mae La camp was one-and-a-half hours. Since the camp was on the early side, we rolled out very early in the morning in order to begin class at eight. The day had grown long whiskers before bedtime in the evening, as we taught for six-and-a-half hours each day, visited a bit with Mr. and Mrs. Simon and some of the students, drove three hours, and had preparations for the next day, as well as eating supper. We filled up eleven- and twelve-hour days and then some. When Fridays arrived, our tongues hung out. We were beat, but with deep satisfaction and unmatched fulfillment.

The teaching conditions in the camp also created challenges for us. Teaching sixty to seventy students (twice the number anywhere else) was the first challenge. The building also required some adjustment. It was a large structure with half-walls made of interwoven bamboo strips. The building breathed and needed to. The half-walls allowed the whips of breeze to slip in and out unhindered. The students' tables were three planks of roughly hewn wood. Their benches were split logs where four students sat. The floor was dirt. We taught from a raised platform and had a large blackboard. Thra Simon translated for all six-and-a-half hours each day. Our clothes stuck to our bodies by 9 a.m. and sweat rolled freely by 2 p.m. each day. Since there was no electricity, there were no lights or fans. We felt like well-done steaks by 4 p.m.

At the end of one week, a group of small children were gawking at our small jeep. Some of them reached out and touched it with glee. Mrs. Simon smiled and explained that none of the children in this camp had ever ridden in a car. We offered to give as many as possible a ride on the following Friday as we finished teaching at noontime on Fridays. After lunch on that Friday, kids swarmed like termites in the teakwood forest. Time after time, we piled little ones—and some not so little— into the back of the jeep and drove them to the paved road and back, a distance of less than half a mile. Such gleeful sounds of joyous hearts experiencing their first car ride would rival any at Disney World. Those sounds and shining eyes have been etched into our hearts forever.

Each time we arrived in the Mae La camp, we experienced "depress-peration." That is, we were depressed by the conditions, but inspired by Thra Simon and the students. There were twenty-five thousand people in houses scattered across a huge valley, like legos that had been kicked apart by a two-year-old. Each stilted house was made of bamboo and had to be rebuilt every three years. The Karens were not allowed to leave the Mae La Valley or work for any of the locals. They lived in subsistent poverty on whatever they could grow or catch. Yet all of them had a forward-focused vision of returning to their homes in Myanmar. Thra Simon had inculcated his vision of raising up an army of the Lord to win Myanmar to Christ into each of his hundreds of students. This vision was vibrantly displayed in each student that we taught. What a privilege it was to walk with one of the true Giants of the faith, Dr. Saw Simon, or better, Thra Simon.

Our joys soared far above any challenges we experienced while at, or while getting to, Mae La camp where we were privileged to stand beside a Giant of a man, the five-foot, four-inch tall Thra Simon.

6

THE MEGA-GIANT
OF HYDERABAD

India is a fascinating study of humanity. For thousands of years, India has produced an amazing race of people. Hinduism, with its inherent caste system, has painted the canvas of Indian society with a very broad brush. Yet the commonplace tolerance exhaled from the vast majority of Indian souls has allowed both Islam and Christianity to stick their respective camel's noses under the proverbial tent of Indian society. I know of no other place on planet Earth where such powerful distinctives have been feathered into the fabric of society, hence producing such an admirable people working together productively. To be certain, there are horrendous exceptions where religious minorities have been horribly slaughtered by the majority religion, but when viewed over thousands of years, these attacks must be considered as a tiny minority compared with the masses who have lived in harmony. The people who have functioned, thrived, and left distinctive fingerprints on such a society certainly should be considered as Mega-Giants. Pastor G. Samuel of Hyderabad is one of those people.

G. Samuel was born on January 5, 1945, and came into this world with "Mega-Giant" seemingly imprinted on his forehead. His father died when G. Samuel was only five years old. His mother, like Hannah of the Old Testament, raised him as a Christian and then dedicated her boy to become a minister of the gospel. By God's grace and power, G. Samuel became one of God's choice servants.

Right after G. Samuel married Eva, they departed for Nagaland, a mission field in northeast India. Concluding three years in Nagaland during which time their first child was born, the Samuels returned to Hyderabad where G. Samuel was called to be the first pastor of Hyderabad Baptist Church in 1970. It was at this church that God started building His Mega-Giant who, in turn, would grow the kingdom of God in such a remarkable way in this city of nearly ten million people.

With one hand in God's hand and the other holding the hands of his developed church leadership team, G. Samuel audaciously led his church to buy a large commercial site in an affluent business section of the city. After prayer-walking the entire site with his team, and then spending a full night with them in a prayer meeting, they decided God was leading them to buy that land. It took every cent that the church had saved just to place the down payment. G. Samuel confidently told the church, "The God who leads is the same God who provides." Such remarkable faith wedded to an astutely gifted mind led the church to pay off the rest of the debt in record time. Again, G. Samuel told his congregation, "Our God wished, our God got. All we have to do is hold onto His hand and do want He wants." Immediately the phenomenal growth began.

Almost twenty years later, G. Samuel invited LEAD to come to Hyderabad and teach his untrained pastors and church leaders. At that time, in 1997, Hyderabad Baptist Church had won and baptized ten thousand people. In fact, in that one year of 1997, they baptized 803 new converts. Some of those baptisms came from their seventy-five mission churches. One in four of those who were baptized originated from an Islamic background.

We were excited to form a partnership with G. Samuel and the

Baptist Church of Hyderabad because it afforded LEAD an opportunity to do exactly what we had been created to do. We discovered that of the seventy-five mission churches sponsored by G. Samuel's church, only ten had pastors who had seminary training, which left sixty-five needing our help. Thirty of the sixty-five that had gone through a year's training provided by Hyderabad Baptist Church. Those thirty needed some help, but that left thirty-five churches who had not been given anything. It was this last group on which we first concentrated.

Another interesting aspect concerning this Mega-Giant was his scope of ministry. G. Samuel functioned at the national level in the organization of evangelical churches all across India. He, likewise, was involved in the calling and training of a rural pastor, like B. Ninay Kumar, who came from a small village in Andhra Pradesh to pastor one of the seventy-five mission churches. Therefore, G. Samuel saw the big picture as well as getting the gospel to one of the poorest sectors of the Indian society that lived in one of the myriad slums of India.

Pastor Kumar and I unwittingly had interesting roles to play in one of God's great teaching moments for the Hyderabad group. Barbara and I had been assigned the Hyderabad LEAD seminar at that time and began it with enthusiasm on a Monday morning at 8 a.m. We were in one of the larger Bible study rooms on the second floor of the education building. It was Pastor Kumar's first LEAD seminar. We got off to a jerky start as Pastor Kumar felt the urge to comment on each point that I tried to make. Since member participation was highly valued in the LEAD seminars, I refrained from trying to control Pastor Kumar in the beginning. However, I was frustrated because I had fallen behind where I needed to be for that day. Barbara experienced the same thing in her class and by the middle of the afternoon class, my patience and smiles were wearing very thin. In fact, they were threadbare. I had tried every trick I knew in teaching to limit Pastor Kumar's interjections. However, there was no way in creation to limit the length of his stories once he launched into one. The group seemed to enjoy them and was all joy and smiles with his participation. At the end of the first day I was livid. I could not afford any more days like that one.

After an evening of cooling off and readjusting some of the material, I energetically started into the second morning. Pastor Kumar was having a ball. For one of the few times in his life he was getting the focus and admiration of respected others. About halfway through that morning's session, I lost it. I spoke harshly and arrogantly. I called this elderly and revered man down like he was a naughty schoolchild. I said, "Do not speak again in this class unless I call on you to do so! We can't afford to waste any more time. Enough!" The effect was instantaneous. Pastor Kumar was grossly embarrassed, which is one of the worst insults any Indian (or other human being) could possibly experience. His head dropped with his chin on his chest and he shuddered away a tear. Pastor Kumar was in his sixties with a scraggily three-day-old beard. He wore a dirty white punjabi with the long shirt coming down to his knees. It was wrinkled and needed to be washed. On his feet were two old and cracked leather sandals that looked to be as old as he was. And he had just been violated by an Ugly American.

The steamy hot room grew icicles. The atmosphere tensed up to the degree that silence commandeered every mouth of the pastors in that room. The thaw never came—that day or the next. Pastor Kumar continued to attend but acted dejected; head down with no eye contact. The learning had stopped and participants were merely going through the motions. Barbara and I prayed.

On Thursday morning, we got started as usual in a frigid atmosphere. Pastor Kumar was in his seat with his head lowered. I told them that I had a statement to make and would appreciate their attention. Many looked at me with a steady coolness.

As I walked up the aisle to Pastor Kumar, I said, "On Tuesday, I committed a sin in here. I spoke rudely to one of our senior and revered pastors, and I am truly sorry." At that point Pastor Kumar looked up into my face. I knelt before him and reached down and put both of my hands on his feet, which was a cultural way of putting myself in submission to him. I then earnestly pleaded, "Pastor Kumar, please forgive me."

He, like a loving father, tenderly reached down and took my hands in his. Then he lifted me up to my feet and said with a radiant smile, "I forgive you." He reached around me and clutched me in a bear hug, and I embraced him back. The room exploded in joyous shouts of, "Amen, praise God!" and, "Hallelujah!" The class surged around us, still in an embrace, and enveloped us with touching, hugging, and joyous laughter. I've never experienced anything quite like it. We finally got back to our studies and it was like an old-fashioned revival. Oh, to be sure, Pastor Kumar continued sharing his stories with us but it didn't matter because God had already taught us the most important lesson, which is, people are more important than lessons. Also, we learned (again) that forgiveness is one of the most powerful elements in the world and can fix any relationship problem.

Today, forty-eight years after the Mega-Giant was called as pastor of Hyderabad Baptist Church, he has seen the church grow upward to almost twenty-five-thousand members. It has been responsible for 19,221 baptisms and started one-hundred-twenty-five branch churches in the greater Hyderabad area. Barbara and I rejoice because we were privileged to work with the Mega-Giant of Hyderabad, Pastor G. Samuel, and also were able to be taught vital lessons from other Giants, like Pastor B. Ninay Kumar. Both of these Giants leave blessed fingerprints (or footprints) on our lives for which we are eternally grateful.

GETTING THERE

Travelling to Hyderabad, India, is easy. Since Hyderabad is considered the Silicon Valley of India, seemingly all roads in India converge in Hyderabad. Normally, we flew Air India to most of our destinations in-country. Then, we typically would pick up ground transportation to the final place of the seminar. Not so in Hyderabad, as the seminar was actually held in Hyderabad. Air India had a program for tourists that allowed people to fly around India for a substantially reduced price. The qualifier was that you needed to fly to five different destinations in India. We, on the LEAD team, more than qualified for that program on each of our teaching treks in India, so we often purchased See India tickets for a very good price. Air India, the national airline carrier of India, was the workhorse of all Indian domestic service. They provided decent service to all of their major hubs, but it was a different story when you used them (or any others) to go to smaller cities. At such times, the service went down like a boulder rolling down a steep slope. We've had Air India flights change the day of departure without any notification. It was all in a day's work to move around on the subcontinent of India.

On one occasion, we flew out of Bangalore, in the south of India, to Hyderabad, situated in the south-central part of the country. We always had two suitcases which usually weighted a total of 115 pounds, or 52 kilograms. Our normal weight allotment on Air India was 22 kilograms per bag, or a total of 44 kilograms for the two. We were always over that allotment. In Bangalore, the official wanted to charge me for the overage. I told that person that I was disappointed. India invited tourists to come and see their intriguing land and persuaded us to buy unique and beautiful objects. When we did, they wanted to charge us extra for being over our weight allotment. The official smiled, slapped a "Heavy" sticker on one of my bags and bid us to have a pleasant trip.

As always, when we went to Hyderabad, we had a very pleasant flight and enjoyed getting to that huge and modern city.

BEING THERE

Being assigned the Hyderabad Baptist Church seminar was the top-rung assignment of all fifty-three locations of the LEAD seminars. Hands down, without a close second, each couple who taught in the LEAD ministry chose Hyderabad as their favorite place to be out of all the other teaching places. This top choice was not dictated by the superior experiences realized from teaching the best group of LEAD participants, although we had some great experiences and notable results from that wonderful group of pastors in the Hyderabad seminars. The number one position of Hyderabad didn't stem from the spectacular vistas afforded the teachers in Hyderabad. Simply put, the motivation of this almost coveted assignment rested on four words: "The Green Park Hotel."

Let me hasten to add a few words of context before anyone writes off the LEAD team as a bunch of hedonistic pansies. Every LEAD couple who drew the coveted prize of The Green Park Hotel had first paid their dues in the boonies for the previous two to three weeks. Most often, the directors of LEAD, who constructed the schedule and made assignments, had assigned that couple to go to Bandarugudem the week before Hyderabad (described in chapter 12: "The Brown Angel with Grit"). The week at Bandarugudem helped to reduce any feelings of guilt of being spoiled rotten in the Green Park Hotel experience. Getting to Bandarugudem required six to eight hours of a sand-blasting road trip, both going and coming. That was the down payment on the "body fee" required at Bandarugudem. The place was always scorching hot or suffocating in mugginess. There was grit everywhere; not dirty, but gritty. You could wipe off a tabletop and within minutes, it looked gray again. The mosquitoes were of the B-29 variety. The electricity was off more than on, especially at night which meant that the little oscillating fan didn't work at all. The cold splash baths, though refreshing, left a lot to be desired for a bathroom experience. In addition, the commode was a squatty-potty. Basically, it was a hole in a raised portion of cement with indentions on each side of the hole to put your feet on. Hence, the name, "SQUATTY-potty," for that's what you did, each time you used it. It got harder by the end of the week as the old Western knees just weren't used to all that much squatting. In all aspects, Bandarugudem was a physically challenging week, especially for us older types who constituted the LEAD team. If you added one or two similar weeks before the Bandarugudem one, then it seemed appropriate to have a luxurious week to follow where everything worked, was clean, and electricity functioned 24/7 which allowed the air conditioner to do the same.

The Green Park Hotel's clientele were prosperous Indian businessmen, wealthy Indian families, and a sprinkling of overseas guests. Often the foreigners were connected to the IT industry there in the IT capital of India. Then there were the occasional Baptist missionaries, like wild-eyed and open-jawed hicks coming down out of the mountains into the real world on Saturdays. We were given this opportunity through the effort of G. Samuel and were blessed by it for years.

Even today, decades later, when The Green Park Hotel is mentioned to a former LEAD couple, a smile slips onto the lips and a deep, deep moan of sheer delight erupts from their spirit. Clean rooms, towels and sheets changed daily, enriched décor, electricity by which to read and study at night, the ability to receive and send emails in our room, no mosquito coils, smoke, or odors, topped by an AC that never stopped and a wonderful bathroom experience all combined to provide the LEAD team an oasis in the desert. Just having hot water—rivers of it—pouring down out of a shower head, created a mountaintop experience. And finally, we enjoyed food worthy of a five-star restaurant anywhere in the States. Heaven came down and touched our spirits during that week. It was a rejuvenating week where our bodies, minds, and souls could be refreshed, giving us the strength to go back into the fray of taking God's Word to those in desperate need who often lived in desperate places.

After teaching in the LEAD ministry for fourteen years, we are convinced that experiences like The Green Park Hotel contributed to keeping a cadre of older missionary couples persevering in many harsh conditions. We were so thankful to a Mega-Giant like G. Samuel, who helped arrange this possibility. He had the vision of not only extending the kingdom of God throughout a megacity of ten million today, but also reaching down into the lowest slum with the gospel. This vision included a way to help a group of God's servants with a respite, readying them to continue going forward with the Word of God for years on end. What a Giant!

7

DOWN THE RIVER
TO FIVE HUNDRED YEARS AGO

The Iban people have populated Borneo since prehistoric man crossed over the land-bridge into what we call today the island of Borneo. This huge island, one of the largest in the world, is divided between the countries of Indonesia and Malaysia. Two-thirds of the island is named Kalimantan by Indonesia. The other one-third, owned by Malaysia, is called East Malaysia and maintains the original name, Borneo. It is the home to some of the most tenacious people on earth, the Iban, a subgroup of the larger Dayak tribe.

Jackson, given the name of Suntai at his birth, and his wife, Seria, are Iban. They grew up on one of the myriad banks of the innumerable rivers and tributaries that make up Sarawak, the western section of Borneo. Transportation for them was by longboat, as there were few roads due to many towns in East Malaysia being water bound. Roads were pretty useless anyway, as the jungle absorbed them faster than the road crews could repair them. Jackson and Seria were native-born to Sarawak and were also young Baptist missionaries from a Malaysian Baptist convention. These young missionaries invited Barbara and me to go to one of the longhouses to hold a meeting before one of our teaching seminars began. Our adventure with them felt as if we floated down the river and back in time five hundred years.

Traditional longhouses in this region are built on stilts about ten feet off the ground. This allowed everything in the jungle to crawl, slither, or pad its way under the house throughout the night. The longhouse walls are usually formed from thatched bamboo. They also have thatched roofs. The houses are set on large bamboo poles or small tree trunks. Flooring consists of interwoven bamboo strips that creaked with every step. Thieves were often referred to as spirits or ghosts because they could move without being heard. Of course, little crawling creatures that played in the thatched roofs day and night often fell out of the roof onto you. Being awaken by a wiggling creature falling on you as you sleep is shocking, to say the least.

In the longhouse where we stayed, there was a hallway that ran from one end to the other. It served as the sidewalk of communal life in the longhouses, which were divided into ten to fifty spaces, much like small apartments. All life flows up and down these hallways that provided shelter from the blazing sun and daily rains. Mothers picked lice from the heads of their small children and nursed infants, fishermen mended nets, and children scampered to and fro with boundless energy. Jackson mentioned that this was where "The Meeting" would take place.

Many of the Iban people had only recently stepped out of total jungle primitiveness into a sub-civilization. Many Iban now lived in these longhouses, adopting more civilized clothing options, and becoming involved in a little commerce. A lot of these changes were purely cosmetic, however, because their hearts were fiercely animistic and rooted in their traditional ways. They believed in spirits, gods, and a host of demons. In their most basic nature, the Iban were survivalists. If anyone hindered or threatened their survival, the Iban attacked, killed, and ate them. If the enemy was worthy, the Iban would cut out that enemy's heart and eat a portion of it raw. Then they decapitated their enemies, shrunk the skulls, and placed them where all could see and take heed.

Through the work of brave missionaries, tens of thousands of Iban had been drawn to the light of the gospel. Some of these Iban fully embraced Jesus and miraculously received Him into their lives. A few of these blessed ones were like Jackson and Seria—saved and called to be torchbearers to other Iban scattered throughout the jungles of Borneo. These Iban, like the ones that surrounded us, were like wild seeds blown up and down the banks of nameless rivers and tributaries throughout Borneo. Jackson and Seria faced a monumental task of starting churches in longhouses, among the people that populated these banks. I likened it to pulling out strands of spaghetti from a boiling pot with a fishhook.

We held our worship service the next evening in the great hallway of the longhouse. Candles and oil lamps provided the light. I had been shocked by a neighbor's front door earlier in the day where he had two shrunken human skulls attached to a stick beside his door. I asked Jackson about it. He answered by saying, "He says it is from his grandfather's day, but everyone knows them to be much more recent. The Iban have killed and eaten their enemies for as long as time has been recorded."

Continuing, he added, "They are probably from the tribe close to the mouth of the big river as they have been enemies for as long as anyone here can remember." I was preaching to folks who looked at the world through a very different lens than any I'd preached to before. However, Jackson had admonished me that they, too, were God's creation and had the same need for His love as anyone from my world. The only difference was they had been blinded by Satan through witchcraft and black magic to the point that murder or cannibalism had become normal.

Jackson requested that I preach a simple message on "Who is Jesus?" There were about fifteen people there who had shown interest in exploring this Jesus thing I shared. We drew a sizable group as we were the best entertainment in town that night. Some sat on the fringe smoking their hand-rolled cigarettes, while others ate rice from banana leaves while joking and laughing. Billy Graham, I wasn't. Enthralled, they weren't. But Jackson said that some truth got through, and for that we praised God.

Then Jackson and Seria broke the group into men's and women's groups. In their heart language, they exposited the verses I had used and took many questions. Barbara and I prayed while the Q&A went on. We both sensed how incredibly intense the spiritual battle was that was being fought all around us. The dark empowerment of evil was in excruciating pain as it was illuminated by the powerful searchlight of God's Word. The name "Jesus" profoundly disturbed them. I could only watch in amazement as these two young Giants battled, tooth and nail, for those precious souls. We were awed by such courage. We were humbled that we could be trusted to "have their backs." These two valiant warriors, who risked having their skulls stuck on some stick beside a doorpost in one of the longhouses, with their chests ripped open and their hearts half-eaten, would not cower, nor would they run off with their tails between their legs. They battled for the most precious thing in life, for an Iban or for us—the eternal living soul. Because they did, there are numerous Baptist churches planted along the rivers and tributaries of Borneo. Only heaven can reveal the final tally of souls that these two young Giants of the faith yanked into heaven.

On the following day, we returned to Sri Aman, a nice, pleasant small town. Then I realized just how big Jackson and Seria's hearts really were. They could have easily made the decision to do ministry there in the town, in relative comfort. But instead they chose to return to those in real spiritual need, knowing full well they were risking their lives for the gospel. These were real giants in the making. I could only stand amazed in their presence and thank God for them.

Getting There

We were getting ready to take the longboats to get to one longhouse where Jackson and Seria were trying to plant a church.

"Don't drink too much, and wear long sleeves and a hat as we'll be on the water most the day," Jackson instructed. He added, "No outhouses on the boat." We laughed. The boat was a forty-foot canoe with two outriggings that kept the boat from overturning. It was powered by an outboard motor but the driveshaft for the propeller was at least ten-feet long.

"Don't hang your hands over the boat to trail in the water, as the crocodiles don't need any more snack food than they already have," came some more instructions, with a slight smile. However, Jackson wasn't jesting. Children and pets are "snapped up" often by the prehistoric creatures and it is a deadly situation to have a boat overturn or sink. Very deadly.

The initial river started out very wide and flowed swiftly. There were no street signs or tributary names posted anywhere. We turned left and then right and then right and then left to find the Engkari River. Only in the mind of the guide did any of it make any sense. About noon we stopped for a little break. The lunch was nice but the outhouse was absolutely fantastic!

The smaller rivers and tributaries allowed us to see the banks more clearly. The green treeline and plant life line came down and seemingly dipped into the water all along the edge. There were a lot of birds, both on the water and along the edge. We saw turtles galore. Some would be sunning themselves on limbs of the low-leaning trees. There were patches of open banks where crocodiles lingered. Most of them were soaking up the rays, but in each case there would be one who paid too much attention to us. Often this one ran off the bank and splashed into the water. His snout pointed at us like he was taking measure on how quickly he could get to us. They were mean-looking critters and they seemed to be everywhere.

We arrived in sweat-stained clothes and beaten to a pulp by the bumpy boat ride when we finally saw our longhouse. It appeared like so many others along the way. There was a clearing about three-hundred feet back from the bank. The longhouse was usually built on a small ridge which was parallel with the cleared part of the bank. The house was rectangular and built on stilts. We were overjoyed at the prospect of getting out of that boat. I envisioned a quick splash-bath and a few minutes rest on a soft bed. Neither happened; however, we had arrived and, for that, we were very thankful.

BEING THERE

The usual ladder, up and into the longhouses, was a large, notched tree trunk. The notches were steps to climb into the doorway of the longhouse. Fortunately, this longhouse also had a set of wooden steps. You entered into a long hallway, which was about fifteen-feet-wide that ran the length of the longhouse. Each "apartment" had its only entrance and exit onto that hallway. This provided for extreme communal living. There were no secrets in the longhouse. There were no separate rooms in the apartments. You ate, slept, got dressed, or undressed for sleeping, all with each other in a great room. Life went on, by some ingenious maneuvers, with and in front of each other. Old people got sick and died; youngsters shared their childhood illnesses with each other; arguments, which at times became fights; and the making of babies all went on in these single rooms of each "apartment."

What a shock it was to a couple of Americans who were raised to cherish privacy. Baths, for me, was in the river, while some boys (or girls) watched for crocodiles, which were never far away. The guys bathed at dusk. There were a lot of comings and goings at that time. My white skin was a prominent point of observation for all. Baths were functionary experiences, not to luxuriate upon. The pointed snouts made sure of that.

Barbara's ordeal was different. They had constructed a bathroom, of sorts, in the middle of the large open room, close to the cooking section of that room. Each apartment was built in the shape of the letter U. The front of the U was the living room, and at night, the bedroom section. The bottom of the U was for storage, both food, tools, and other things. The back of the U was for cooking and food preparation. Then it doubled as the dining room. The area in the middle of the U was an open-sky area that allowed rain to pour through and also a place that food debris could be tossed down on the ground, under the longhouse. Of course, that is where the pig pen was. This open area was also the logical choice for an "indoor bathroom." They had bent two pieces of tin around three poles. There was no door, just the ends of the attached sheets of tin, which made an awful noise every time you moved it. There was a hole in the middle of the bathroom floor for drainage and other business. Again, when the tin was moved, an announcement was made to the world that someone had just entered the enclosed room. The following water noises made sure that all knew what you were doing in that enclosed room. It seemed like forever between sunset and sunrise the next morning for a couple of us. As stated, there are no secrets in longhouse living.

We slept on a thin mattress put on the floor with a "grandma" extremely interested in our white skin. She found it to be hilarious. She also slept on part of our thin mattress as it was the only one in the room.

They told us about the fifteen-foot-long boa constrictor they had gotten to eat the week before. It had come in at night, killed and eaten one of their pigs kept in the pen below the house. The problem was the snake could not get back out of the rock fence with the newly devoured pig in its gullet. They had a feast and ate both the boa and the pig.

The meals we were served were also unique. There were no pieces of furniture in the room, so the kitchen table was the place where we had walked to and fro during the rest of the day. We sat on the floor in a circle. Everyone could reach into a common pot placed in the middle of the space. There was a huge shiny head of a catfish looking up with pale eyes and its mouth open. Everyone placed some rice in a bowl, splashed some broth out of the common bowl, and pinched off a piece of slimy flesh from the catfish head. A few veggies were in a big bowl, such as jungle weed, which tasted exactly as you would imagine jungle weed to taste. It didn't matter, because they had already put a lot of fiery hot peppers in and on everything. While we ate, the host of our apartment said, "Oh Brother Bush, since you are our honored guest, we are saving the most delicious part for you." He then proceeded to pluck out one of the catfish's pale eyeballs and plopped it in my bowl. As soon as I understood what he was about to do I tried to dissuade him with, "No, no that's OK; I'm just one of the family, huh?" It didn't work. As everyone watched and licked their lips in anticipation, I had to slurp up the eyeball, smiling all the way. That is when the missionary prayer comes in handy, which is, "Lord I'll put it down if You will keep it down."

It was a long trip "down that river to five-hundred years ago," but we were so privileged to see a couple of young Giants hatchetting a hole in impenetrable darkness so that the gospel light could shine through. Truly, it was a lifelong blessing.

8

THE LIFE-LIFTING GIANTS

Adam and Elia Sandepudi saw a living demonstration of a radical change of life when their parents received Christ as their Savior. The Sandepudis joined millions of others who lived on the sidewalks of a large city in India. Life on the streets of India was usually pretty short. The family put all of its income into buying food for daily survival. Every day young Adam, senior by two years, took his younger brother, Elia, by the hand to search for something to eat. As young as age six and four they went into the local marketplaces where they spied out rotten vegetables such as cabbage or green beans that had been tossed on the ground. The Sandepudi boys would snatch these up and run home with their contribution for the one meal the family would eat that day. Hunger gnawed at their little tummies every day and through most nights.

Sometimes, as a family, they went to the local dump. These were not Waste Management Systems! These were DUMPS; no management and certainly no system was involved. They were huge mounds of garbage. The stench was so unbearable that even as little kids they tied dirty cloths over their noses and mouths. These were disease factories with their own transmitting system—huge black flies. These buzzing black flies were not easily intimidated. After all, this was their domain. But the saddest fact was these mountains of garbage were also children-eaters. Often, a small child fell into a wormhole running downward from the top to the bottom of the mass of garbage. These were beggar children. No expense was wasted on them by trying to dig them out. Adam and Elia were familiar with the animal-like shriek; the mournful scream of a mother fruitlessly trying to dig out one of her little ones with her bare hands.

The common question is, "Why take such risks?" The answer is simple; the dump is comprised of garbage from the general society, which breaks down to 1 percent filthy rich people, 18 percent well-to-do middle class, and the rest mired in poor abject poverty. Therefore, 18 to 19 percent of the garbage offers true treasures to the extremely poor. These treasures are things to sell in order to buy some food for that day. Or there might have been some delicious food stuffs thrown away the day before, tainted only by the filth in which it is discovered. The Sandepudis, like other gut-wrenching, extremely poor families, were master survivors.

Miraculously, Adam's and Elia's mother and father heard and believed the gospel. They embraced Christ with a desperate and eternal clasp which could not be broken. Along with some immediate perse-cution came enormous blessings. Habits changed in both parents that led to using more of their meager income for the betterment of the family. Then a big blessing came. Mr. Sandepudi was given a regular job in a store owned by Christians. That meager, but steady, income brought transformational changes to the Sandepudi family. Adam and Elia went to school for the first time in their lives. Adam often stated that the first pair of shoes he ever owned were those bought for him to attend school. The required school uniforms had to be washed every night, at first, because they could only buy one set for each boy. All of these experi-ences were foundational, as God built two special Giants for His work.

The two brothers grew up in the grace of God. They were able to get a high school education and were blessed by scholarships to attend a Bible School. As the potter shapes his vessel by applying pressure with his hands on certain parts of the turning lump of clay, so God did likewise in the lives of Adam and Elia. They became His workmanship as they dedicated their lives to serving God.

First, God led them to establish an orphanage in Visweswaraya Puram. The name of the town was bigger than the small burg that it was, but that was not important to the two brothers. What was important was that God had provided a parcel of land just outside of Visweswaraya Puram on which the Sandepudis erected Dayspring. In Luke's Gospel, Zacharias refers to "Dayspring" with the meaning of "Dawn; The Messiah." Adam and Elia planned for Dayspring to be the spiritual dawn for hundreds of children who were either fully orphaned or had only one parent. The brothers vividly remembered how drastically their lives changed when their parents encountered Jesus. They remembered clearly what Jesus had done in their own lives when they, too, accepted Him as their personal Savior. Joy, peace, and a manageable living had replaced despair, gloom, pain, and constant gnawing hunger. Instead of searching in stench-filled mounds of decaying garbage for bare subsistence, they looked up and found a loving heavenly Father who gave them a blessed life. This was going to be afforded to every child that God gave to them.

Adam married Mary Helen and together they handled much of the ministry of Dayspring. They made contacts, both internationally and locally, to raise funds for buildings and for supporting the growing number of kids that wanted to come to Dayspring. Elia and his wife took charge of the construction phases and the day-to-day operation of the ministry. A third brother, born after the parents' conversion, was named David Livingston, after the famed missionary to Africa. David and family likewise joined the ministry team. He focused on connecting Dayspring to local ministries, both in gathering financial support and in providing spiritual training opportunities for local pastors and cell-group leaders. The Spirit of God was working and numerous house churches began to pop up all around Dayspring.

The living conditions at the orphanage would most likely have appalled childcare workers in the United States. Each child slept on a thin bamboo mat with the padding of a thin blanket. Every child's total world's goods fit inside of a tin box about the size of a shoebox. Their sleeping compartments slept twenty-five children and had one low-wattage lightbulb for each section. But despite the meager conditions, Dayspring had grown to one-hundred-thirty kids, with a waiting list of scores more clamoring to get in.

Why?

It is because each child was fed three decent meals a day. They were guaranteed the opportunity to attend school through high school, and were taught to be responsible, as each child had chores to do every day in order to maintain their living situation. Also, they were loved by godly substitute parents. Each child was cherished and celebrated as he or she grew toward adulthood.

LEAD was asked to assist in the second part of the plan that God led the Sandepudi brothers to accomplish. They wanted to assist in planting new churches throughout their district in Eastern Andhra Pradesh. Adam and David found almost twenty pastors and lay-pastors around Visweswaraya Puram who were interested in receiving Bible training from LEAD. Barbara and I launched the first LEAD seminar at Dayspring and were overjoyed at the potential represented there. We adjusted times of the seminars to coincide with the school break periods. That way we used the orphanage facilities to house and feed the participants. The chapel became our study room which worked well. God blessed, and the seminar attendance grew steadily. In fact, within five years we had to add a second LEAD seminar to accommodate all who wanted to attend.

After three years of LEAD seminars, I remember one occasion that illustrated how God used the Sandepudis to flesh out the gospel in that area. We reviewed the subjects that had been taught in the previous seminars which were held six months before. One subject was "Church Planting." I asked how many new churches had been planted, thinking how great it would be if there were three or four reported. To our utter amazement, that group of twenty-three participants had planted nineteen "porch churches." That meant that nineteen new worship services were being held under the roofs of nineteen houses. Stunned, I asked how this happened. "Well," they answered, "we just did what Brother Tom (Tom Barron, the LEAD teacher in the previous seminar) said to do, and God did the work." Not all of the nineteen fellowships survived, but most did, with three or four of them building new small buildings in which to worship. The kingdom of God grew and much of it was because The Potter had shaped two brothers (and eventually, three) into worthy vessels through which He could pour out His Living Water.

Adam continually tried to get more money out of LEAD's pocketbook, not for himself, but for the Dayspring children and for the young untrained pastors. I understood his heart. Elia, quiet, like a well-tuned engine, got things done more smoothly than anyone could have believed, given all of the challenges of caring for more than one-hundred children. And David Livingston did honor to his namesake. These brothers and their wonderful wives were huge Giants of the faith, reaching down to orphaned kids, the most vulnerable in their society, and then reaching out into a lost community with an effective gospel. We were always humbled by each and challenged by all.

GETTING THERE

In the first years, getting to Visweswaraya Puram was a major challenge. The trip was about as long as the name itself. LEAD teachers flew into Hyderabad and caught a night train going eastward toward the eastern Indian coastline. The train travel alone took approximately eleven hours. After boarding our train in Hyderabad around 9 p.m., we would stagger off in Rajahmundry about 8 a.m. Eleven hours on an all-night Indian train seemed close to a lifetime. However, the real lifetime would be experienced on the return eleven hours back to Hyderabad, especially after spending five days and nights in Visweswaraya Puram.

Before boarding the train, we had to bargain with the porters to carry our two substantially heavy suitcases onto the train. We could have physically handled our own baggage, but it would have insulted the working class of Indians that depended on that work for their survival. However, they never made it easy.

"Five hundred Rupees," the porter offered boldly. I'd sputter like I'd lost my breath, and recovered a bit to counter: "Maybe fifty Rupees for each bag."

"Oh, Sir, how can we live on such a miserly amount?" pleaded the porters; always three or four in a group. About that time, one began to rub his gaunt-looking stomach and added, "I haven't had a customer all day long, so I haven't eaten anything today. Maybe I could carry one bag for two-hundred Rupees?" By that time we had become a mini sideshow. I knew the Indian price for my bags should between one hundred and one-hundred-fifty Rupees (about two dollars) and we always added our "skin tax" on top of that.

"Okay, because it is late, I'll make this final offer. I'll give you two-hundred Rupees for the two bags. Tops!" I said with all of the finality I could muster.

"Two-hundred-fifty and we'll do it, Sir, even though that's a pathetic little for us," They squeezed out hopefully.

"Okay," I agreed, confirming with a wave of my head. "But I'll pay you on the train." They all agreed with that similar sideways motion of their heads. Then two well-fed men stepped up from the back of the crowd and hoisted the bags on their shoulders and marched off to the spot where our car would be located. I grabbed our computer bag while Barbara held on firmly to her purse and a briefcase as we followed our bobbing green and yellow suitcases through a sea of people to our waiting spot. It was worth the four dollars just to be in that proximity so that we could easily step up into the correct train car when it arrived.

We always rode Second Class, which meant we had one-half of a compartment. In each compartment there were two long, padded benches facing each other. We usually were not able to communicate very much with our Indian neighbors, just share a few tidbits of information and smile a lot because of the language difficulties. But it was usually a pleasant and friendly experience. Indians can be some of the most gracious people on earth and we were normally treated with kindness and respect unless we were bargaining with them. From the first lengthy train trip, we were instructed first by a conductor and then by traveling Indian companions, that we absolutely had to buy a chain and padlock to secure our luggage while on these trips. This was doubly emphasized for overnight trips. So, as soon as the porters placed our bags under the long bench we locked both of them with a chain and lock. Thievery wasn't invented by Indians, but the Indian train thieves will match any others in the world. We kept the other two bags against the window side of our seat and never left them alone no matter how strong the urge was.

At night, the cushioned backrest of the bench seat slid up and flattened out into an upper bunkbed. I would put the two bags up there, crawl in beside them and try to get some sleep. The rickety sound of the tracks matched the bobbing of our heads and our feet, like we were in a rowboat in the ocean. It made some sleepy, while making others seasick. There were thin blankets handed out that were actually useful as a cover or a pillow. During the night, if one of us needed to use the restroom, we woke up the other.

No one had to tell you where the toilet rooms were located because you could just follow your nose. The septic tank smell filled the small rooms themselves and then seeped out into the rest of the train car. The toilet rooms were a specialty of their own. Keep in mind that these trains rocked side to side every moving moment. Some of our LEAD teachers actually got seasick while riding these trains. Another factor to keep in mind is that these toilet rooms have no commodes. In the place of a commode was a raised metal plate with a hole in the middle of it. There were imprints on each side of the hole to indicate where you should put your feet as you squatted over it. You noticed, right away, that there was no holding tank underneath the hole. You could see the railroad ties flash by underneath. However, the trick was maintaining your balance as the train rocked, sometimes jolted, back and forth. Many did not maintain their balance which caused them to miss their target. It was a messy business, especially for us uninitiated Westerners. This experience taught us bowel discipline like no other lesson we'd ever had.

After we arrived in Rajahmundry the following morning, we still had a one-and-a-half hour car ride to Dayspring. One of the Sandepudi brothers gathered us up and transported us to Visweswaraya Puram, which would be our home, temporarily, for another week. It was so welcoming to get on solid, unswaying land again and to be able to relax a bit before we started teaching the next morning.

BEING THERE

Being with the three Sandepudi families was like being at home. They yearned for us to feel at home with them and we always did. Mary Helen fed us until we could eat no more. She kept insisting we needed to keep up our strength. Many times she filled our plates before we were called to the dining table knowing that we knew, culturally, it was an insult not to eat all of the food that was on our plate. With a wry grin playing around her mouth she said, "Just so you can serve the Lord more." Who could refuse that?

The precious family devotion times with about seventy of their kiddos was a taste of what heaven must be like. The other children had returned home for the school break. The devotion time was held in the chapel with all of the chairs removed. We all sat on the floor and some of the smaller ones sat on us. With our ears, Barbara and I had little understanding, but with our hearts we fully understood it all. There was a lot of singing with hand-holding while swaying with the rhythm of the guitar. Laughter erupted from time to time so that we'd have to start the song all over again. Peals of delight created more smiles and more laughter which in turn brought on another wave of it all again. During each evening's family devotion time, there were no rigid time restraints. We all gathered after supper and the evening sparked alive with singing. There were elements to the time, but not a lot of structure. Always included during this time each night was singing, praying for those who were ill or hurt, a devotional thought shared (not a sermon), and sharing experiences of the day which God had blessed. At the end of the time, there was a quiet moment; a moment of contentment. Night after night, we were privileged to share in an intimate touch of God. Those family devotion times were worth the price of the ticket and far beyond it.

Only true Giants of the faith could have created such a rich atmosphere—Adam and Elia, who had experienced the powerful hand of God lifting them out of despair and dumps of their life into His heavenly presence. Only they could grab ahold of so many little hands and lift them into that safe, peaceful, and joyous atmosphere at Dayspring. His Giants could do that; no one else could. We are forever grateful God allowed us to walk with all three Sandepudi families who are true Giants in our eyes.

9

HEART-SHAPERS
IN A HARD LAND

In northern Pakistan, life is bedrock hard. The rugged terrain adver-
tises that death triumphs over most living things there. People who
survive in such environs reflect their harsh realities. It takes tough hearts
even to survive, much less to actually thrive. Therefore, for those who
are going to shape the hearts of these rugged people, they must possess
a granite-like commitment with no reverse gear in the transmission of
their heart. There are two such persons I'd like for you to meet.

Ifrahim Akhter Matthew was born in a staunch Muslim family.
They lived on the edge of Islamabad, the capital city of Pakistan. Ifrahim
melded into the routine of a Muslim's life where making multiple trips
on a daily basis to the local mosque was as normal as eating chicken
karahi, chased with a lassi, a delicious, soothing drink made from sweet
curds. During Ramadan, the Muslim's fasting month, Ifrahim's family
suffered. They took it to heart and did not eat or drink anything from
earliest light until hard dark each day. They did this as a daily testimony
to their devotion to Allah. Both of Ifrahim's parents set high standards
in all of their commitments to the prophet Muhammad's words.

While in high school, Ifrahim's world greatly expanded. He was
exposed to different ideas even though they were posited to him with
Muslim cushions. It was there that he met a Christian teenager who

possessed a different perspective about the prophet Isa (Jesus). Over a period of a couple of years, Ifrahim examined the Christian message and its Messenger. As a result, Ifrahim made a choice that significantly altered the rest of his life and eternity. He received Christ as his personal Savior and promptly lost everything else dear to him.

Shortly after high school graduation, Ifrahim told his family about his new understanding concerning the prophet Isa, who he now knew as Jesus the Christ. Their reaction was swift and decisive.

"Recant or get out!" his father demanded. Ifrahim left his house, his community, and his city. Like most Muslims who lived in the rigorous northern part of Pakistan, when they became believers in Christ, they had to flee to the South. There are Christian enclaves in southern Pakistan, even in the megacity of Karachi. Arrangements were made and Ifrahim joined an adopted Christian family in the southern part of the country. He learned a trade, got married, and then God called him to be an evangelist back in the rugged regions of northern Pakistan.

God had honed his servant, Ifrahim, to be a very sharp tool in the hand of a skillful Master. God gave Ifrahim brokenness through the loss of his family. He led him to be penniless and, therefore, dependent on Him alone. God also installed in Ifrahim a fearless heart. Being totally committed to his Heavenly Father, Ifrahim was a "one-God man." He backed down from nobody. He was thoroughly equipped to take the powerful gospel to the hardened souls of the North.

Ifrahim was a hard man among hard men. He developed a strategy to distribute Bibles and Christian literature that was unique to his environment. It required men and women to be rock-solid in their commitment to their Lord Jesus Christ with an unequivocal faith in the power of God's Word. Matthew was one of those who had been won to Christ by Ifrahim and then trained to use this very different strategy. With Ifrahim, God grew a Giant with broad shoulders and a blunt head as His ideal instrument for sharing the gospel in that unfor-giving terrain.

Matthew is the second Giant from northern Pakistan whom I want to share as he adopted Ifrahim's unique method of evangelism there. Matthew was born as Sadiq Masih and took the name of Matthew when he was born again. He had opened the New Testament and discovered the name of Matthew before any others. He said, "I chose that name because it was the first name in the Gospels, and I want to be the first to take the gospel to my kind of people."

Matthew did that week by week in the upper regions of Pakistan by hawking Bibles in the midst of a different marketplace each week. Matthew's team understood that bazaars were the synapse of Pakistani life. These marketplaces were where life flowed through the arteries of every community. The richest households, represented by servants, down to the street beggars, all trudged through the lanes of produce and products in these bazaars. Both the absolute essentials were there in addition to items for the wishlist.

Ifrahim's strategy consisted of teams composed of two men and one woman. There would be teams assigned to various bazaars around Islamabad and extending northward. Often members of these teams would also be interchanged to insure no one returned to the same bazaar within a couple of years. It would be too dangerous if they did.

After prayer and fasting for their assigned bazaar, the team arrived about midmorning, insuring crowded conditions. Matthew had surveyed the place where he would put up an aluminum, fold-up bookrack which displayed his Bibles. It took only a couple of minutes for setup or takedown. Then he scanned the crowd for his target. There would be one or more in each bazaar. These targets were those who were there to be seen as well as to purchase something. He tagged these individuals as peacocks. These men wore their superior religiosity in their white, flowing robes and gleaming turbans. An entourage would be quickstepping a few paces behind each of these peacocks. Matthew would lock onto one and boom out in a loud voice: "Hey, you in the white robe, wouldn't you like to buy a Bible?" He held one up and stared at the man.

The target would be very predictable as he made an abrupt turn and sneered. He answered Matthew in the most derogatory manner possible, calling Matthew every lowlife name that could be used publicly. The game was on. Understand that in Pakistani society, especially in a bazaar, boisterous, argumentative voices were as common as women having their heads covered. Matthew and his target squared off about fifteen-feet apart. As the white-robed one shouted his slurs at the Bible seller, Matthew answered each one by shouting out a step of the plan of salvation from the Bible. No one ever noticed that Matthew never countered the vicious attacks on his character or his religion but matched the heat of his antagonist by shouting out the Roman Road plan of salvation, or some other biblical presentation of the gospel. He shouted them one step at a time in between each visceral verbal attack on him, as though he were answering his attacker, tit for tat. Sometimes he got to insert an invitation or even a prayer to receive Christ. Hundreds of Muslims heard the gospel in an acceptable form of Pakistani communication, week after week.

Matthew knew the signs. He had learned when to start packing up his display so that he would not lose his Bibles or stand. He normally could tell when the bazaar police would appear and was ready for them. The cost of admission would then be extracted. The police came and beat him with batons. They kicked him when he eventually fell below their blows. Then they dragged him out of the bazaar to the entrance where they threw him in putrid slush where the dirty vegetables had been washed before market opened that morning.

His team was alert. They retrieved him when things settled down a bit. They ministered to his cuts, cleaned his scrapes, sometimes bound his ribs, and prayed. Within half an hour, one or two inquirers often appeared where Matthew had been tossed. If it was a woman, then the woman on the team went to meet her. If a man, then the other man on the team went. Sometimes these inquirers were only mildly interested in who this Jesus really was. Others were ready to receive Him and commit their lives to following Him. The team answered all questions and led those who were ready to make a commitment to Christ to do so. Follow-up appointments were made, if possible, and instructions on where to find a local group of believers were given.

Matthew and others on Ifrahim's teams added to the kingdom of God, one cracked rib, one cut brow, or one broken wrist at a time. Ifrahim, Matthew, and their teams are among those to whom the author of Hebrews referred when he wrote, "… of whom the world was not worthy." We were honored to be selected by God to strengthen these Giants with His Word. As this team sat in front of us with their scarred faces advertising the high cost of serving Him in that hard land, we were truly humbled to stand in their shadows and serve them as they served Him.

GETTING THERE

Each trip to Pakistan was an adventure and always provided plenty of reasons for prayer. Our schedule remained the same each time. We flew into Karachi and conducted our first LEAD seminar there. Then we flew to Islamabad and took a chartered twenty-five passenger bus down to Jhelum. The trip from Islamabad to Jhelum was usually about three hours, though at times it felt more like ten hours. Each trip was rife with opportunities that could have prevented our arriving at all. But by His grace, power, and much prayer, we arrived each time.

One predawn morning, Naveed, our colleague and coordinator for the Karachi LEAD seminars, took us to the airport in Karachi. We were headed to Islamabad. Traffic was sparse at that time of morning. We talked about our seminar and our anticipation of being with Ifrahim at the Jhelum seminar, as his team usually rode down to Jhelum with us in the bus. I was aware that we had caught more red than yellow on a couple of traffic lights. Then we blatantly blew through a red one without even slightly slowing down. I joked about not having enough rupees to pay for a red-light violation. Naveed laughed, but did not say anything until we got to the airport. Then he explained that recently there had been a rash of violent robberies at a number of the stoplights we just passed through when people stopped for the red light. After the explanation, Naveed grinned and said, "But we didn't have to make any red-light donations, did we?"

We were met at the airport in Islamabad by our LEAD coordinator for the Jhelum seminar. He was a local Baptist pastor in Islamabad. He got us a taxi to the ancient city of Rawalpindi on the edge of Islamabad. There the bus collected us, Ifrahim's team, and a few others, to travel to Jhelum on the three-hour trip that would take us over some mountains and then down into the lowlands.

On this particular trip the bus was late. We had used this same company for the past two or three years and had always been satisfied. Upon arrival of the bus, we loaded all of our gear, luggage, and stuff on top of the bus where it was covered with a tarp and tied down. Then the bus lurched into the city traffic. From the very get-go there was a noticeable difference about the way the bus was being driven. It was the usual rat-race getting out of the cluttered city. We, however, cut people off more sharply than ever before. The medium-sized bus repeatedly pushed its way into holes only big enough for motorcycles. The squawk of angry horns and screech of complaining tires constantly assaulted our ears until we got out on the highway headed toward the mountain ranges. Some of us were openly vocal in our disapproval of the way the bus was being driven.

Once on the open road things deteriorated. Sixty mph was usually the top speed for those two-lane highways, and we well exceeded that. Our bus came screaming up behind slow moving trucks or buses, and then whipped out into oncoming traffic, forcing them either to hit us head-on or run off the road onto dirt shoulders. Some of us began to shout at the driver to slow down but that only aggravated the problem. Just as we started up a long grade into the foothills, our bus ran up behind a long line of semi-trucks, all nose to tail. Again, the driver jerked the bus out into the oncoming traffic. Barreling down the slope toward us was a semi-truck, kissed by a bus behind him. There was no room on the shoulders, as it sloped downward from the paved road. As we braced for a head-on collision we saw the semi flash by right beside us and felt a wave from the compressed air between the two vehicles as there were mere inches separating us. By God's immeasurable grace, in a space sufficient for only two vehicles, He managed to squeeze three large ones.

Then, when we were certain that things could not have gotten worse, they did. Coming down the other side of the mountain, the driver went squealing around each curve, especially the hairpin ones. We had come up on a blind curve when the driver saw another slowly moving bus in the middle of the curve. He yanked the steering wheel and lurched our bus to the inside lane only to find a semi-truck directly in front of us, entering the curve from the opposite direction. Again, I can't explain the physics of how three solid objects were pressed into the actual space of two. Both of the other vehicles hit their brakes and pulled toward the outer edge of their lanes while our driver hit the gas and sliced in front of the bus in our lane. We literally saw the faces of both drivers that reflected shock and explosive anger as they wrestled with their respective vehicles.

After arriving at the Shalom Retreat Center in Jhelum, the driver jumped out of the bus and ran off somewhere. We were then informed that our regular Christian driver was sick and this was a substitute. The coordinator suspected that this driver was on some kind of opium, as are many long-haul drivers in that part of the world. We just praised God that we had arrived safely, again by God's grace.

BEING THERE

Jhelum, Pakistan, in February or March can be chilly, requiring a blanket and added hot water for the splash baths. But in September, it is just plain hot! No hot water is needed. The rooms are spartan, but do have a ceiling fan which is a life sustainer. There is an extra bed on which to place stuff, also some small shelves are available. The bathrooms have Western toilets with toilet paper provided. Splash baths feel good as you pour the water over you from a cement tank. Mosquito coils are a necessity. There is a large desk available which serves well for studying or computer work. All in all, the Shalom Retreat Center is an excellent place for a LEAD seminar.

One memorable LEAD seminar at Shalom was held September 10-14, 2001. I was alone, as Barbara had returned to the States to attend the birth of a grandchild. It was the first time either of us had gone home for a special event and we were so excited. I had asked Naveed Malik, our LEAD coordinator for Karachi, and an outstanding translator, to accompany me to Jhelum and teach the course of Personal Evangelism, which is what Barbara had been teaching. I taught the book of Psalms and the course on the Holy Spirit.

We got off to a good start on Monday. Then on Tuesday, just before supper time, Edwin, Shalom's manager, came rushing in and told me that America was being attacked. In my patronizing voice, I said, "Edwin, it's just a movie. America's not being attacked." He responded about the reality of it and asked me to come to his house to see the

HEART-SHAPERS IN A HARD LAND

TV program. I agreed in order to settle him down. Naveed and I went across the street to his house and entered just in time to see the second plane hit the Twin Towers. "Wow," I exclaimed. "They have made it look very real, you know, with real CNN reporters and all." However, within a few minutes I realized what Edwin and Naveed already knew: it was for real. I was stupefied.

Edwin brought his TV over to the dining hall so all the participants could see what was happening. About 8 p.m. that night, I walked out of the compound to a local private telephone kiosk to call my father on his 83rd birthday, which was also on September 11. He knew where I was and repeatedly said, "Just get out of there, right now." I answered him that I was in good Hands.

On Tuesday evening we heard guns being fired into the air as celebrations broke out all over Jhelum that "The Great Satan" (USA) was being brought to her knees. Revelers drove up and down the main street of Jhelum, blowing their horns, crying out, "Allahu Akbar!" ("God is great!") throughout the evening. At breakfast time on Wednesday morning, September 12, I received official instructions from our mission organization to evacuate Pakistan. I was told that the United States may bomb Pakistan if they were complicit in the attack on the Twin Towers. I told my supervisor that I understood his message. He pressed the urgency of the situation, but I could not immediately comply. I was teaching men and women who bore multiple scars on their faces and bodies for sharing the vital message of God's Word. I was teaching them about the powerful messages from David's book of Psalms and about the victorious works of the Holy Spirit. How could I negate those truths by fleeing because my life might be in danger? Their lives were constantly in peril.

Naveed and I agreed that I would teach three sessions a day for the next two days and be ready to leave on Thursday afternoon. By that time Edwin was concerned that there might be an attack coming on the compound, as I had been seen in town on Tuesday evening. Edwin bought me a plane ticket from Lahore, Pakistan, to Bangkok, Thailand, leaving on Thursday night. Then he secured a safe transport to drive me from Jhelum to Lahore. I left shortly after dark on Thursday and drove straight to Lahore with no stops, arriving about 9 p.m. It was chaotic at the airport, with military surrounding the entire complex. Westerners were trying to get out of Pakistan. I was on the plane by 10 p.m. and in the air an hour later. When I arrived in Bangkok I was informed that I was on one of the last flights out of Pakistan before they closed all airports at midnight on Thursday night. "Thank you, Lord," was all I could say.

Standing shoulder-to-shoulder with men and women who often put their lives on the line for Jesus was such an unmerited privilege. Knowing these committed souls would die for one or two of their countrymen made my decision much easier. It was not a matter of courage as much as did I truly believe the Word of God, and were these brothers and sisters worthy of my death? My immediate answer was, "Absolutely!" I was just following His example, and theirs, and would not hesitate to do it all again today.

10

AN HONORED GIANT
OF THE HILLS

The Khond Hills of Orissa, India, have been the home of the Kui People for centuries. Since ancient times, Satan has whispered into the hearts of the Kui and they have responded. They have had intercourse with evil through the ages, delving into the worship of spirits, powers, and idols, while prostrating themselves before certain caves, beside special rivers and on top of select mountains. They had no better choice until the British came and brought Christ displayed in white buildings and through strange-sounding music, along with other traditions.

It was in Mallikapuri, just a wide place in the road running through the Khond Hills, where the very first Kui became a believer in Jesus Christ. Poto Prodhan was baptized into the membership of the Mallikapuri Baptist Church organized by British missionaries. Then in 1947, the British pulled out of India after India won its independence. By that time, Poto was joined by a host of other Kui that worshipped God in that Baptist church.

It was a wild land, consisting of layers of peaks and valleys, where Bengal tigers roamed free. Most of the cultivated land, hacked out of the jungles, produced an abundance of food except during the dry season. The term for "dry season" and "hunger," in the Kui language is the exact same word. In spite of many challenges, life went on and the Prodhans produced a child. He was given the name of Paul. Paul's life was vastly different than that of his parents'. He grew up loving Jesus Christ. He and his siblings, though a small number among the Kui People, found that worshipping God in their church two to three times a week brought deep comfort and satisfaction. Paul grew up in that small town at the head of a gorgeous valley between two distinct hills, got married, and had children. They all attended that same church in which his father was the first Kui to have been baptized.

There was a power vacuum when the Brits left. Chaos became the norm as various factions vied for leadership roles. Evil struggled for thrones. In fact, the last record of human sacrifice among the Kui took place about two-hundred yards from the Mallikapuri Baptist Church building. As usual, a young and pure little girl was slaughtered like a ewe lamb and then sacrificed on a fiery altar ignited by flames from hell. The Prodhans may have witnessed it as it was so close to them. In retrospect, it should surprise no one that Satan chose that spot in Mallikapuri, close to that church, to make a desperate lunge for power. He probably could sense the increasing power of the Holy Spirit in the hearts of the growing number of believers there. In its early stage, Satan tried to abort this power of the Holy Spirit, but failed.

Poto called his son Paul to his deathbed in 1955 to charge him with an immeasurable task. Poto said, "Son, the Brits have gone and taken all of their missionaries with them. I am dying, so I charge you to win our people to the Lord Jesus and start churches up and down this great valley."

Paul responded by declaring himself unfit for such an enormous task. He could have said that he had never studied in seminary, much less taken the course, "Church Planting 101." He had never studied anywhere but in his own living room as he read his Bible, often by candlelight.

But Poto answered and said, "Paul, why do you think we named you Paul? There are no other Pauls in our family. We named you after the apostle Paul. Therefore, you will be the apostle Paul to the Kui People; to our people."

At that time, Paul Prodhan was a moderately successful business man. He sold tea leaves both in Mallikapuri and in villages in the hills lying on both sides of the valley. There were almost no roads but only footpaths that linked the interlaced farming villages throughout those hills. Paul and Mrs. Paul began using those same trails to take the gospel to the Kui. They would often sit by the water wells and sing Christian songs. If any were interested, they would share about Jesus and offer to come and explain more in their own homes. They also offered Bible lessons on how to follow Jesus.

Of course, not everyone was happy with the Prodhans. Paul and his wife were often assaulted by fanatic Hindus. Sometimes an irate husband would attack them for "changing" his wife. Many times, because of these beatings, Paul and his wife would limp back home where it would take a week or two for their wounds to heal. Then they would get back on the trails so they could reach one more Kui, maybe one more village. By God's grace little pinpricks of gospel light began to dance in the cruel darkness surrounding Mallikapuri. House churches began emerging in village after village. Paul became exhausted pedaling his bicycle up and down those rocky pathways endeavoring to lead Bible studies and preach in as many churches as he could.

On one occasion, Paul was late for a worship service being held in one of the first church buildings that had been built in the entire valley. It was dusk and he was pedaling as fast as the rocky terrain would allow when he saw a shadowy lump ahead in the path. Suddenly, the lump moved. That striped lump moved gracefully to its four feet and fixed an eerie stare upon Paul. Paul came to a sliding halt and fell off the bike about twenty feet from the large and curious Bengal tiger. The tiger slowly moved into a crouch while never averting its eyes from Paul. For some unexplainable reason, Paul picked up the bicycle and held it up sideways in front of his head and shoulders. According to Paul, the big cat then stood up, shook himself from front to back, turned and trotted off down the trail and eventually bounded off the trail into the forest. After Paul got his heart slowed down a tad, he thought about rushing back home. But then Paul considered that if God had spared him from becoming supper for the big cat, then surely He desired Paul to continue on to the church in order to share His Word with them. So he ventured on to the church. Later that night, Paul returned back along that same trail.

It surprised no one but Paul himself that God chose to use him and his wife in extraordinary ways. Thirty years later, when we met this legend, he and his loving wife had planted scores and scores of churches that had in turn planted hundreds of other churches. Associations of Baptist churches had been planted and they were moving toward forming a full convention of Baptist churches. All of this happened because this one untrained man and his small wife were faithful to keep on going down a rough and rugged trail not only to preach the gospel, but to be the gospel. The apostle Paul Prodhan was truly an honored Giant of the Khond Hills.

GETTING THERE

Travelling to the state of Orissa, India, is similar to a trip to West Virginia. We did not find high-end, expensive stores or five-star eateries outside of the capital city of Bhubaneswar. Like in West Virginia, we found goodhearted people struggling to make a living in a nearly exclusively agricultural-based society.

We flew into Bhubaneswar and overnighted at the New Kenilworth Hotel. The main reason for this selection was that a part of the "New" was the installation of a backup generator. Like many major cities in

India there are periodic sessions of electrical blackouts which are rotated systematically through various sections of the city. The New Kenilworth's backup generator could handle the electrical load of lights and fans, but not the air condition system. So when our part of the city was in the blackout mode we could still read and study. We would not start to swelter until about three hours into the blackout. By then our rotation would almost be over and the blessed cool air would soon be seeping back into the room.

The prearranged transport company had a car and driver waiting for us on Sunday morning about 9 a.m. The trip from Bhubaneswar to Mallikapuri took approximately five hours if all went smoothly, which it rarely did. For example, our colleagues, Gerald and Brenda Burch, had recently made this five-hour trek in a record-breaking seventeen hours! Since the drivers spoke virtually no conversational English, we traveled a lot by faith. The destination was always communicated in written form so as to eliminate misunderstanding of our mispronouncing the name of the city or village. The Burches questioned their driver about the route as nothing seemed familiar to them.

"No problem, no problem. Just a little more," came the continued answer. After about seven-and-a-half hours into the supposed five-hour trip, the driver pulled into a tiny little burg and announced, "We arrive." But they had not! After driving to a nearby town that had a telephone office, the driver called his office. At the end of a lot of shouting between the driver and his office, Gerald got on the phone and was informed that the driver had misinterpreted the written name and had gone to the wrong village that was "Just a little out of the way." They piled back into the car and travelled another ten hours before they entered the small town of Mallikapuri at about 2 a.m. Six hours later, Gerald was standing in front of about thirty-five farmer/pastors ready to teach God's Word to them.

Thankfully, our trip to Mallikakpuri went smoothly this time. We arrived at Cooper Cottage, our abode while in Mallikapuri, by midafternoon. The trip had been uneventful, which was always something for which we thanked God. There were many lovely vistas through the mountains, and the pastoral setting of Mallikapuri warmed our hearts and soothed our souls. We were "at home" for the next five days with people we loved and greatly admired from the Khond Hills. We were in the huge shadow of "The apostle Paul of Khond Hills." There was no better place to be at that moment.

BEING THERE

When we arrived, our hearts calmed to a slower rhythm to match the pastoral surroundings where cows and goats dotted the lazy countryside. Most houses were made of mud and straw with thatched roofs. Cooper Cottage was built on the far edge of the Mallikapuri Baptist Church property. Everything was great except for the fact that we were missing the smiling face of Paul Prodhan. He had always been a part of the picturesque scene in Mallikapuri, and was usually sitting on the front porch of Cooper Cottage when we arrived. But Paul's health had been failing for some months and his gigantic shadow was fading into the twilight of his life. He was home in bed being nursed by his loving wife.

Owen Cooper was a devoted believer from Mississippi. He was also a fertilizer magnate and had gotten involved in the Khond Hills where he would eventually locate the first nitrogen fertilizer plant in India. While there, he ignited gospel projects which aided the church planting results from the Prodhan's productive service. Since he spent so much time in Orissa, he built a small cottage that he used while staying in the Khond Hills, and also made it available to Christian workers. The cottage was built in the late 1960s. In 1973, Mr. Cooper was elected as only the second layman ever (non-clergy) to become the president of the Southern Baptist Convention. In the 1990s, LEAD began teaching the fruit of the Prodhan's harvest which was aided by Owen Cooper's efforts.

The cottage was known as Cooper Cottage and had grown older with the wear and tear of service for more than thirty years. The cement floors were cracked and potted in places. The two bunkbeds per bedroom were utilitarian with lumpy mattresses. Of course, there were no screens over the windows or doors, because why would anyone want to keep all of those flies and other critters inside? At least that was the prevailing attitude of the locals. There was no running water unless a younger man carried the water pails instead of an older woman. However, there was intermittent electricity; off more than on, especially at night.

The bathrooms were special; one large and one small that only had a commode and a sink. The smaller had a "high and lifted up throne" where even people who were six-feet tall or taller could barely touch the floor with their toes while sitting on it. The large bathroom also had a commode but was set very low to the floor. The porcelain rim functioned as the seat and was about 18 inches off the floor. You flushed both with a dipper from a small water tank built beside the toilet. Toilet paper was only available if you bought some in the capital city and carried it with you to Mallikapuri. The bathing facility was also a larger water tank with a dipper so that you could pour water over your body, soap up and then rinse off. We called it a "splash bath." Of course the water wets the entire floor and drains out from a lower corner of the room which had a hole built into the wall about the size of your fist. There was always a rock placed close to the hole in order to stop it up at night, preventing the creepy-crawly creatures from entering. The rock was usually forgotten which facilitated some interesting stories throughout the years.

As the story goes, the McAtees and Wortens were the two LEAD couples teaching that week. After a candlelit supper (because the electricity was off) both couples prepared for the next day via oil lamps and flashlights. After all had gone to bed, Carolyn McAtee arose in the night to use the bathroom. The small oil lamp flickered out enough light in the bathroom to move around in it. Suddenly with a bloodcurdling scream, Carolyn shouted, "Jim, get a light and come here! I've just been cold-nosed." Jim got his flashlight, stumbled into the bathroom and shined his light down into the toilet only to find two beady eyes staring back at him with a twitching nose. The large rat hopped out of the commode and scurried out of the room via the hole in the wall.

During our week of teaching we visited our friend, the Indian apostle Paul, two or three times to pray with him and his wife. He was in bed covered with a couple of blankets. We wiped sweat from our faces but it did not matter as we were in the presence of Giants. Their bodies were played-out. They had left it all, not on some silly ballfield, but in the field, where the harvest of souls came at a high price—their own health and lives. We all felt like we were being knighted in some royal court when Paul placed his feeble hand on our shoulders, and his wife cupped our hands with her bony fingers and prayed for us to be effective as we taught "their harvest."

Such simple prayers wrapped God's grace around our necks like a mantle; prayer that had the power to push dark, spiritual mountains away and shackle demons away from us. It was the last time we saw Paul and Mrs. Paul on earth, but it won't be the last time we ever see them, for we shall see them in heaven. They are going to be the ones with neck braces, as their crowns will be too heavy for them to bear. It won't matter because they will just take them off and place them at the feet of Jesus where they had placed each and every day of their lives while here on earth. It was one of our highest honors to have walked in the shadows of such great Giants of the hills.

11

THE SEASIDE NURTURERS

Marten and Femmy Adaling had already lived a lot of life to be only in their early thirties. Marten was the coordinator for the LEAD seminars on the island of Halmahera, in the northern Maluku islands of Indonesia. He also supervised all the Baptist work accomplished on that island for an Indonesian Baptist convention. This island is perched on the outer rim of the northeastern boundary of that island nation. Although the number of islands in Indonesia exceeds seventeen thousand, Halmahera apparently holds significance to Satan, as he has tried more than once to take it by force. Twice, Satan instigated island-wide attacks by Islamic warriors from neighboring islands. Marten and Femmy experienced one of those attacks in 1999 before they were married, and were barely able to catch a large boat sent to rescue Christian survivors. All of those survivors escaped to Manado, a predominately Christian city on the island of Sulawesi. It was in that traumatic situation that God opened their eyes to each other. Soon afterwards Marten and Femmy became Mr. and Mrs. Adaling. Not long after that blessed event, and after the Indonesian army took control of the situation on Halmahera, the Adalings volunteered to return to Halmahera to continue their work there. One part of their assignment was to supervise the work of planting and developing Baptist churches across that expansive island where 50 percent of the inhabitants were

Muslim and the other 50 percent were Christian.

When the Adalings returned, they chose to live in a Muslim neighborhood. Marten and Femmy wanted to show their Muslim neighbors the love of God, thereby proving to them that Christians posed no threat to their Muslim neighbors. It took over a year of being ostracized, called hurtful names, and periodically having garbage thrown in their yard before any of their Muslim neighbors warmed up to Femmy or Marten. The Adalings continued to smile and greet each of their neighbors warmly every day during that first year. While picking up the garbage strewn over their yard, Marten and Femmy sang hymns and peppy spiritual songs. The end result came when the woman next door almost died. Femmy took food, cared for the school aged children, and even did some laundry. And prayed! Femmy's neighbor got well and the relationships in the neighborhood thawed. Afterwards, kids played in the Adalings' front yard after school every day where pisang goreng (fried bananas) or some other snack was found. Likewise there were often some neighborhood mothers and grandmothers found in Femmy's kitchen where good stuff always happened. Not to mention that during the afternoon coffee time, kopi tubruk (aromatic, thick coffee) awaited all who stopped by. Femmy was a great cook and even greater hostess. Femmy had won first their stomachs, and then their hearts to her side, where her neighbors wanted to be, especially in trying times. Within two years a number of the Adalings' neighbors whispered discreetly to them that Marten and Femmy never had to fear an invasion again because the attackers would have to go through these dear Muslim neighbors and that just would never happen.

Marten and Femmy oversaw the organization and execution of our LEAD seminars in Tobelo, Halmahera, and did it with precision. Femmy took charge of all food production. The ladies from Zion Baptist Church, where Marten was pastor, assisted her in every way. The meals were rice-based, simple, and mouth-wateringly delicious. They were also *pedas* (spicy hot)! No self-respecting sinus cavity could remain closed after taking just one bite of Femmy's cooking.

Many of the participants of the LEAD seminars were freshly graduated seminary couples in their first real ministry position. Most were struggling with culture shock even though they were all Indonesians. There were vast differences between ethnic groups that populated those thousands of islands. Marten and Femmy were the perfect couple to compassionately, but firmly, guide these young couples to grow into productive pastors and church planters. Baptist churches began growing on that battleground island.

One gigantic challenge for Marten was getting adequate medical care to his shepherds. Many of those Baptist pastors lived along the shoreline of Halmahera which was accessible only by boat or a motorized pontoon canoe. There were no internal roads, therefore no easy access to a doctor or hospital. Another great challenge was dealing with the lack of funds. Very little money was available in those mission churches after paying the ministers' miniscule monthly salaries. Funds were not being mishandled; there just wasn't enough. Marten did what he could by getting a few donations from more affluent churches in town when a crisis occurred. These valiant giants of the faith went out to the far-flung places, merely niches in the virgin jungles, and planted their lives, sometimes unto death.

Yuryen and Sumi, with their young son, Adi, exemplified that truth. They lived in one of those jungle niches about four hours down the seaside from Tobelo. Yuryen owned a small boat that allowed him to fish in order to augment the small monthly stipend he received from the Baptist convention via Marten. Yuryen and Sumi had started a small, fledgling Baptist church in their village. When they needed to shop for anything it usually required a two-day boat trip to Tobelo and back. It took four hours each way. They would shop and then overnight with the return on the following day. It was costly both in time and money. Yuryen could barely bounce alongside the coastline because his outboard motor was so small.

One day Yuryen returned home from fishing ablaze with fever. He spent a couple of days alternating between being on fire and seemingly being enveloped in arctic air. He'd sweat rivers of water then bury himself under a blanket with spare clothes placed on top of the blanket, all of this in a sweltering jungle setting. He had contracted malaria! Although quinine had been around for more than sixty years, it hadn't yet gotten to Yuryen's and Sumi's village. He could have bought some in Tobelo but that required the long boat trip. Then Adi began to exhibit his dad's symptoms, alternatingly shaking with chills and then burning up with fever. Mom and Dad held him and prayed. On the second day, early in the morning as the sun fluttered its eyelashes over the horizon, Yuryen was holding his son when the boy began to breathe raggedly. Adi was already limp and the color of chalk. His little eyes beheld his father and then closed. Adi labored through a couple of gulps of air and just stopped breathing. He died in his daddy's arms.

After burying their tiny son that morning, Yuryen and Sumi limped over to Tobelo and into the arms of their spiritual Giants, Marten and Femmy. The Adalings lovingly, patiently, and compassionately repaired this broken mom and dad. It took weeks, but eventually Yuryen and Sumi wanted to return to their village and their church. God had used two special Giants to forge two younger Giants of the faith. In the following years, many couples who had suddenly lost children were assisted back to health by Yuryen and Sumi.

In a land before quinine (or much else, medically speaking), God prepared giants to face the most desperate circumstances. These giants spoke authentically from knowledge, not theory. They could effectively show others God's eternal plan that could issue forth hope even in the most hopeless cases. Like Marten says, "When we gain God's eternal eyesight and understand that He wants each of us to be with Him in heaven for all of eternity, then any investment is worthy, either His son or ours."

GETTING THERE

Consistently getting to and from Tobelo, Halmahera, Indonesia was our greatest travel challenge in the entire LEAD ministry. We could fly into Manado, the modern capital city on the island of Sulawesi, with no problem whatsoever from anywhere in Indonesia, or even from out of the country. The challenge came when we tried to go from Manado to Tobelo. The best option was to fly from Manado to the small, but influential town of Kau, Halmahera. Then we traveled by car to Tobelo, which took about ninety minutes. But the greater obstacle was reversing the trip back to Manado because the small plane would often be cancelled in Kau. There were a myriad of reasons offered for the cancellation, including weather, maintenance problems on the aircraft, and maybe snowballs on the potholed runways. Well, snowballs might be a slight exaggeration, but some of the reasons came pretty close to it. So we could get in, but it was much more difficult to get back out. When the flight of the twin-engine, twenty-seater, super Piper Cub plane was cancelled in Kau, we had to go overland across the island and then cross over a strait on a ferry to Ternate. Then we dashed from the harbor to the airport in hopes of catching the next plane flying from Ternate to Manado. It was a six-hour trip with opportunities galore that could cause us to spend the night in the transport car. Flooded roads, in the rainy season, a collapsed bridge or an overturned truck in the middle of the two-lane road could double those hours. Every trip to and from Tobelo exercised our prayer muscles to the point of pure fatigue.

On one occasion Barbara and I boarded the small plane in Manado.

I called it the "rubber-band plane" because it looked so tiny that maybe a rubber band could turn the propeller. The weather was blustery with intermittent rain. We sat in the front of the aircraft, right behind the cockpit. The canvas seats were wallowed out and my seatbelt latch was broken. I tied the straps together. In the place of the door to the cockpit hung a dirty, paper-thin curtain. It was shoved over to one side. Of course there was not a stewardess so the copilot took our tickets and saw that everything was stowed properly under our seats. There were no overhead compartments. We soared off of a wet runway and climbed into a gray, weeping sky. As the heavens darkened with a frown, our spirits dampened into a sense of foreboding. Rain pelted the glazed portal pane beside Barbara. The ocean below seemed to be washed away with a driving rain. We could see nothing but drenching water gushing downward from a sinister black veil covering the entire sky. Neither could the pilots see anything, as we were looking through the open door and out their windshield. After about an hour of being buffeted about by what seemed to be a gigantic heavenly firehose, I saw one of the pilots stand up and look downward out of his front window.

That is when I got very concerned and doubled up on one of those missionary prayers: "Lord it's us again. We are in one of those predicaments again. Please help us." Not long afterwards, the nose of the little plane started to dip. That gave me the opportunity to see clearly through the front window as there was a circular hole in the dark clouds. Quickly we zoomed through it, which revealed an island which had a tiny runway on it. The trouble was that the runway was doing the jitterbug because of the movement of the plane, which was dancing one way and then the other. I grabbed Barbara's hand. The landing was going to be rough, if at all. We prayed harder. The plane hit the runway nearly sideways. The pilot fishtailed that little aircraft down the soggy runway and brought us to a stop in front of the terminal. Inside the plane was an eruption of clapping and cheering. As the pilot came out I congratulated him on getting us safely back on the ground. He smiled and mentioned something about having plenty of practice as he did one of those about once a month during the rainy season. Wow! We were in good hands and even better Hands.

The headaches were plenty but the blessings were far more. Being able to teach Giants like Marten, Femmy, Yuryen, and Sumi, plus so many more made all of the challenges pale into insignificance compared to what God did through His servants there in Tobelo and throughout Halmahera.

Being There

After overcoming the array of challenges to get to Tobelo, being there became the crown jewel of all LEAD seminar places. Our accommodation at the President Hotel was top notch. It even had AC, at least while the electricity was functioning. Our second story room provided a spectacular view of the small port with a panoramic scope of the South Pacific, dotted by numerous green isles. Outrigger canoes to small passenger ships ebbed in and flowed out during the days while we were in town. The hotel even provided pastries and coffee every morning for breakfast as well as aromatic afternoon coffee for the one who was not teaching the afternoon session.

We rode pedicabs back and forth from the church on most occasions. It was a five-minute ride or a fifteen-minute walk. The people were friendly and our being able to converse in the Indonesian language was a gigantic plus. After fifteen years of previously doing church planting on the islands of Java and Bali, Indonesia, the language, food and customs were very familiar to us.

The Zion Baptist Church hosted the LEAD seminars and was the church that Marten pastored. It also functioned as a training center for

Baptist church programs and continuing education for Baptist pastors and church planters; hence the LEAD seminars. Marten had the gift of administration which was clearly reflected in the way our seminars were so smoothly conducted in Tobelo. The food, produced by Femmy and the church ladies, was scrumptious. We ate mostly fresh fish caught in the early mornings with an occasional meal of chicken sate (meat skewered on sticks) layered with a rich peanut sauce. All of this was put on top of a bowl of white rice that also included a variety of cooked veggies. Each bowl then was topped with a sinus-clearing hot chili paste made up of fiery hot peppers.

One of the last times we taught in Tobelo I came down with a rare case of diarrhea about midway through the week. We always carried Pepto Bismol, which took care of most cases. When it didn't, we also had some Lomotil which solved the most severe problems. I continued teaching my sessions with a few spontaneous break times. On Thursday I had to switch to the Lomotil. Still, I was able to persevere and continue teaching.

Around the grounds, there were always animals wandering about, with some coming in to investigate what was going on. There were dogs, cats, roosters, and occasionally a swayback pig or two.

One younger dog had been tied to a tree in the side yard. I had petted it for a day or two. I assumed one of the pastors was taking him home after the seminar. That Friday, Barbara and I both taught morning sessions. Then we concluded the seminar at lunchtime in order to give the participants time to start back home. Friday lunches were always a bit more special as we celebrated the ending of a precious time together in God's Word. On that particular Friday, the class informed us that this meal was very special as it was one of their most favorite foods. We had not had beef all week long, so I thought maybe we were going to have steak. We ended the last class and shared our genuine appreciation for all of the hard work done that week. We had the closing ceremony and were dismissed in prayer, which also included a blessing for the favorite food we were about to partake. Before we sat to eat, I made one quick trip to the bathroom. When Barbara and I went out the side door we suddenly realized what their favorite meal was. The skeletal ribcage of the dog was lying on the ground where it had been tied, as if it was ready to fetch a ball. The furry skin was off to one side. We knew that we were about to eat a special meal of anjing (dog). I made a dash back to the bathroom.

When we entered the room where all the food was arranged on the tables, Barbara and I saw something we'd never seen in Indonesia. It was black rice. We commented to each other that maybe it was a special rice to accompany a meal of dog. One of the church ladies then came through the room with a cloth draped over the back of her neck. She used it to dry the sweat off of her face, wipe things off of the tables and to wave it over the food that might have attracted some flies. At that very moment we realized that the black rice was, in reality, white rice totally and completely encased with large black flies. It provided another opportunity to pray another common missionary prayer: "Lord, I'll put it down if You will keep it down." Miraculously, He did.

We often realized that there were many differences between us and the seminar participants, such as language, food choices, and skin color. But our unity in love for the Lord Jesus Christ and His church created such a powerful bond that no such differences could ever really unlatch our heart-cords from one another. We were all one body, His Body, and that superseded everything else. The bonding with Giants such as Marten, Femmy, Yuryen, and Sumi remains one of our most cherished possessions.

12

THE GIANT'S GIANT

At forty-three years of age, Ajen was the mature Giant developing other spiritual giants in the Karangan area. Karangan is a narrow place on a slender, two-lane, paved road cutting through the interior of West Kalimantan (Borneo), Indonesia. Borneo has always been a tough place to live; wild and out of control. With wild beasts, suffocating heat and a nearly constant 100 percent humidity in sweltering jungle conditions, Borneo has spawned more diseases than doctors have been able to name. In such a place, Pastor Ajen soared far above merely surviving; he planted and developed church after church. For sixteen years, he and his family fought through devastating diseases while at the same time defeating powerful spiritual foes. Ajen shined the gospel Light on souls chained in darkness so they became unbound people, free to reach their potential and free to create thriving, prosperous communities.

Pastor Ajen and his compassionate wife, Ibu (Mrs.) Ajen, effectively shared the gospel in one village where the Lord used them to win and baptize 50-60 percent of the village. At that point, the Ajen's Baptist convention sent a freshly graduated student to pastor and lead that church, after which Ajen and family moved deeper into the interior and did it over again. God protected Ajen and his family and honed him into a spiritual Giant who became an overseer to assist many others who were walking, literally, in his footprints.

After those sixteen years, his Baptist convention asked him to move to a less vulnerable area of service in order to multiply younger servants of God who would minister in those desperate conditions. Ajen was asked to pastor the Karangan Baptist Church, which was one of the largest churches in the whole area. It had been started by Canadian missionaries who had also constructed the large church building. Truly, it was a prized position and perfect for a Giant-maker.

The Karangan Baptist Church was the site for our West Kalimantan LEAD seminar and Pastor Ajen was the coordinator. His masterful leadership was fruitful because he could get the pastors of so many of the interior churches to come, and a few of them would bring their wives. Not only did they receive beneficial training, but Ajen and Ibu Ajen could counsel many of them during the times when they were not in class. God used these mature Giants to raise up a number of younger Giants that had great influence on large swaths of this huge, untamed, and unevangelized island.

Let me share accounts of two of Ajen's younger Giant families.

Pastor Ajen informed me about Brother Wahet's situation as to why he would not be attending this LEAD seminar. The young couple had married immediately after graduating from the Baptist seminary and moved from the capital city, Pontianak, to a nearly prehistoric village. It was a shock and had presented a major challenge to both Wahet and his new wife. But in the shadow and nurture of Pastor and Mrs. Ajen, the Wahets made considerable strides forward, both in their young and tender marriage, and in their effectiveness with the gospel. Pastor Wahet baptized nearly half of his church members after he arrived. They had made significant advancements against the spiritual darkness that surrounded them.

He and his young wife were ministering in one of the deeper, interior churches that had a thatched bamboo-walled building with a thatched roof and dirt floors. At this particular time, Wahet's wife was at the end of her first pregnancy and Wahet decided he was needed with her much more than at the seminar. We all agreed with that decision. There were no roads where the Wahets lived, only a few trails and a large river flowing by the edge of their village. Nor were there any stores, doctors, schools, or hospitals; only the Wahets, along with about twenty church members out of the one-hundred-and-fifty people of that village. There were, though, several older women who functioned as midwives, although they had no formal training.

We remembered the Wahets in our prayers during the seminar. We finished with no word from them and headed to the next LEAD seminar on a different Indonesian island. Barbara and I were in transit when we got Pastor Ajen's telephone call. He had travelled to the closest city with telephone service in order to reach us. Tearfully, Ajen informed me that Mama Wahet had died while giving birth to a precious baby girl. As Mama took her last gasp of breath, the baby took her first.

"Awww!!! How could God let this happen?" I screamed in my heart as I tried to speak a few words of encouragement to Ajen and a promise of prayer to Wahet. My dear, dear brother Wahet. He was so unprepared in every human measurement; education, spiritual maturity, financial— in every way.

Barbara and I were both shocked numb. As we sat in that airport waiting room, the Lord spoke into my heart. He said, "Who else can shine so effectively in such darkness as one unprepared? Strengthened by My love and comfort, he will be able to share My message of love and salvation to those who surround him better than any 'prepared' messenger. Living in the interior, how many more 'Wahets' are going to need My Authentic Voice to bring true comfort and then salvation?"

Then the Father added, "By the way, I'm in the same place that I was on one Friday afternoon when My only Son died on a Roman cross. I was brokenhearted then as well as now. His suffering was for all. Wahet's suffering is for some who will only come to Me by such an experience." I cringed when I felt His next words to me, "Are you willing to suffer for Me to reach even one more?"

I was crushed. The enormity of eternity came crashing down on my soul and I knew that I'd gladly surrender my paltry few years of so-called life for just one person to be drawn into an eternal, blissful relationship with the Heavenly Father. I also caught a glimpse, in my mind's eye, of Pastor Ajen and his loving wife becoming the face and hands of a loving God to Wahet. What a Giant!

The other account about Giants-in-the-making concerns Akip and his wife Sumi. They started attending the LEAD seminars in Karangan as single young people before God led them to become husband and wife. Sumi joined Akip in the interior church that he was pastoring. Their village was prosperous. There was one dirt road and a small river connecting their village with others. There were a few shops and the beginning of an elementary school. Akip and Sumi both were gifted leaders and soon they had won and baptized most of their village. Akip was training a young seminary graduate to take over for him. He and Sumi, following the pattern set by Ajen, the Giant, were preparing to move somewhere more interior and do it all over again. But first they would come to the LEAD seminar, bringing with them their eight-month-old daughter who was sick. Mrs. Ajen took care of the baby while Sumi was in class. Akip and Sumi stayed with the Ajens as there were no more private spaces up in the house where the rest of us lived for that week.

On Wednesday, this fine couple requested a meeting with Barbara and me. We chose the longer break time between the last class and supper time. They told us of their decision to go to an extremely remote village up a major river into one of the most primitive areas in all of

Borneo. Both Barbara and I responded, "What? Are you crazy? You can't take your baby to an area like that."

Unfazed, they both answered, "But God has called us there. We cannot not go." The matter was settled in their hearts and minds. We tried to be sensitive to their sense of leadership from the Lord but still needed to confront them with the realities of that decision. We spoke to them of having no doctors available to them or their baby. We reminded them that schooling would also not be available for their children as there were no schools within a day's travel from that place. There would be no electricity for probably years to come. There would be no refrigerator, no shopping, no occasional break such as eating out, or any such things. But they countered with the fact that there were more than two-hundred lost souls in that village with only one known believer. They would go!

It was a six-hour trip up a large river until they came to a thousand-foot waterfall. There they would have to exit the boat and carry all of their belongings up a trail beside the waterfall, then get back in a different boat and go another four hours before they reached their new home. Akip and Sumi went home after the seminar to pack what they could carry in a motorized outrigger canoe. They would leave in the morning after they said their goodbyes to the church. On the Friday after finishing the seminar, we had a commissioning service for Akip, Sumi, and their baby. After much prayer, some weeping and laying on of hands, we sent them to follow God's will. As they departed, they said we would not see their faces again. They were right. None of us ever saw them again. Periodically Pastor Ajen would receive word about them and then there was none.

I cannot describe the ultimate sense of privilege that we felt standing in the shadows of these younger Giants, much less the Giant that God had given to them. We taught them God's Word but they taught us how it should be fleshed out with the expected cost of obedience. The enormity of eternity never seemed clearer than in those days.

GETTING THERE

The "cowboys" who piloted the planes in Indonesian airlines, especially the privately owned ones, were usually quite adept at keeping their horses in the air. For all domestic flights, we flew Indonesian airlines as we did to Pontianak, W. Kalimantan (Borneo), and always managed to arrive safely.

Rev. Sperry usually picked us up from the airport. He was one of the very few that had access to an automobile. Sperry was the president of a Baptist seminary in Pontianak. The school was well-funded from abroad and produced some outstanding servants of God. They fueled the leadership for most of the struggling Baptist churches of the interior. These young graduates were thrown into the fray of leading barely survivable jungle churches, where they expended boundless energies in life-and-death struggles. Some of these struggles were metaphorical while others were in flesh and blood. They immediately faced rampant and devastating diseases and serious lack of financial support, while living on an emotional roller-coaster. At the same time they had to fend off the demons that constantly howled at them from spiritual darkness. They were Giants-in-the-making and Pastor Sperry held their lifelines which were often attached to his heart.

The conditions at the Baptist seminary were very comfortable. It was a great launching pad to the interior LEAD seminar and even a greater retreat when returning. Sperry met us at the airport on Saturday and then transported us to Karangan after worship on Sunday afternoon.

The trips usually were uneventful, in answer to fervent prayer. They were successful because Sperry was an excellent driver, knowing when to pass on narrow two-lane roads, knowing when to move over and let the large trucks own the middle of the road and knowing when and where to stop for potty breaks.

As we pulled out of Pontianak, we could feel the modernity of civilization ebb away in our rearview mirrors. The land was delta for miles and miles. Canals cut patterns in the earth like a patchwork quilt. Gaunt men plodded along side of the road in their faded shorts, shirtless, topped with a plaited straw hat. Life was hard here; truly hard.

The closer we got to Karangan, the small towns became fewer and fewer. Daily items that were needed became weekly or monthly ones for which to be shopped. Life pressed out the "want" into the form of absolute need. Those living in those conditions would constitute the bricks and mortar of His Church in this land. It took Giants to do that hard work. Likewise it took a mature Giant to meet the needs of the younger ones in training. They would be planting churches in some of the blackest spiritual holes of darkness on earth. That mature Giant among younger Giants was Pastor Ajen, and we always looked forward to seeing his smiling face each time we arrived in Karangan.

BEING THERE

Being in Karangan afforded us some unique opportunities as Barbara and I lived with twenty men in an old house when we were there. The house had been constructed by a Canadian Baptist missionary couple who had lived in it while doing church planting ministry around Karangan. They also built the church building that was now the Karangan Baptist congregation. These were thirty-year-old buildings but in decent shape. LEAD used the church building to teach all of its seminars for the pastors who served in the interior of Borneo.

Living with twenty men gave us keen insights as we got really up-close and personal with all of them. We also experienced them in all stages of dress and undress, especially during the morning and evening bath times. There were four bedrooms plus a helper's room into which we all were shoehorned. The house also provided two bathrooms for all of us to use. Barbara and I had priority on the larger bathroom from 6-6:30 a.m. every morning so we could be ready to teach at 8 a.m. Since we preferred taking our baths just before bedtime, we had no problems with lines at 9 p.m. The only big challenge came when someone came down with a case of diarrhea, which could be caused by a number of factors. When that happened we all went into a creative maneuver mode.

Our small bedroom was about eight-by-ten-feet, with one constantly opened, unscreened window. We had a curtain for privacy. It was a one-track room, which meant only one of us at a time could move around in the room. The bed was up against the wall and one person had to get into it from the foot of the bed. We had a small closet for hang-up clothes and one small rack with four shelves. In the daytime we tied a rope from the open rafters, which went cattycornered across the bed, in order to dry our towels. The room was snug, but doable.

We needed to use mosquito coils throughout each evening. The mosquitoes came in two varieties, big and gigantic. The bigger ones seemed to have snouts about the size of elephant trunks, or so it seemed. The prize possession of the entire complex was the stand-up electric fan in our room. I am certain it saved us from drowning in our own sweat more than once. Unfortunately, since Karangan was in a rural area the electric company rarely fixed any problem that occurred at night. In those instances we'd fan each other or use a damp towel in order to cool ourselves.

At night we were usually exhausted and fell into a loud slumber pretty quickly. Occasionally, when we didn't, we heard little scurrying feet above our heads. From time to time I shined my flashlight up into the exposed rafters and saw long-tailed rats making their journeys from one side of the house to the other. Actually, they were very good tightrope walkers, worthy of being circus performers, as they never fell one time in all the years we went to Karangan. Of course, that fact never prevented our periodic thought: "What would happen if they did fall on us while we were in bed?"

One of the scheduled LEAD seminars each year occurred in the rainy season. That season was rife with challenges. Rivers of water could pour from the sky, much like a large waterfall on a sizeable river. The rain came thundering down so loudly that we often had to stop teaching for a while. Sheets of water were so thick we could barely see the church building from the old house merely thirty yards away. Sometimes these sheets of rain drove sideways, which would flood any room with an opened window or door.

Moving around in the monsoon-like rain was always precarious. We guys rolled up our pant legs, held our flip-flops in one hand along with our Bibles and notebooks, and went sloshing and sliding down the muddy pathway to the church. Barbara and I always carried umbrellas, but none of our participants owned one. So after we got to the church building, the umbrellas would be used to ferry the rest of the gang to the church building in clumps of two or three. Pastor Ajen usually had a towel to use, which helped the first few. After all arrived, we got started with no lights as the electricity in the rainy season was off more than it was on.

The food in Karangan was always good even though the meals were always rice-based meals with little meat provided. Pastor Ajen's wife, often called "Ibu Pendeta" (Mrs. Pastor), did an outstanding job of supervising the food preparation. As usual for that part of the world, the kitchen was located in a separate, three-walled building built from thatched bamboo and close to the rear of the house. Any Stateside food inspector would have a heart attack over the unhygienic conditions in which that good food was prepared. The animals, dogs, piglets, and chickens would occasionally wander through the kitchen. Scraps were often tossed to the dogs who were never far away during cooking times. Of course, they would never allow all of those flies and other flying critters to be trapped inside by installing screens in the windows. Therefore, there were plenty of those varmints available to cover any of the food left uncovered. Then there were the dishtowel-like cloths that each cook used to wipe utensils, spills, and occasionally a sweaty face. These all contributed to the robustness of that good food. Karangan wasn't for the tender-stomached people of the world.

All in all, it was a high honor to stand beside such Giants, both the matured and maturing ones. Some of these were Giants because of the stupendous results they achieved or events they endured. Others achieved Giant-hood because of their big, broad spiritual shoulders that muscled-up remarkable loads day in and night out. Ajen was one of the latter ones. We always admired him and his wife for the constant source of strength they provided for those who struggled in the interior and for us who were privileged to walk along side of some of them.

13

A GIANT IN THE SLUMS

Mumbai, formerly known as Bombay, India, is a city of contrasts. There are two parallel universes fleshed out among the fourteen million people in that megacity. One universe claimed, in the 1990s, that more millionaires lived in Mumbai than in any other city in the world. The second claimed the largest single slum of any city in South Asia. This particular slum has spawned scores of smaller ones splattered throughout the expansive city of Mumbai. Therefore the filthy rich constantly jockeyed up against the filthy poor. All of this is mediated by pure greed on one side against a life-and-death struggle for survival on the other. So it shocked everyone when a man named Stephen, having one of his feet in the first universe, decided to stick his other foot in the second.

Stephen, his younger brother, Sudhakar, and two sisters grew up in comfort in Mumbai. Their family was in the 18 percent middle class of India, which meant that they enjoyed a standard of living similar to most Americans. Stephen and Sudhakar were on the track to take over their father's position as a merchandizer. He acquired materials such as vegetables, hemp, and bamboo from the countryside. With skill he prepared them, packaged them, and distributed them throughout the metropolis of Mumbai. But then God upset the applecart.

Sudhakar stated it like this: "My brother, Stephen, got changed. Then I got changed. Now all my family got changed." Stephen had "got changed" by the gospel of Jesus Christ. One of the merchants to whom Stephen had made deliveries had an attractive life and family. Because of that Stephen had little resistance in accepting an invitation to a service at a small church in a poor neighborhood nearby. He went. And went again. Shortly afterwards he "got changed" by asking Jesus to forgive him of all his sins and come into his life and live there.

Within a year, God whispered in Stephen's ear, "I want to love 'them' through you. Will you become my servant?" Stephen immediately surrendered everything—his heart, his mind, his ambition for affluence—everything. A radical decision produced radical changes that produced radical results. Sudhakar and his sisters followed quickly. Within two years Stephen's whole family had become devoted followers of Jesus, not just pew-sitting Christians. Not long after that, Stephen's Mom and Dad got involved in that poor church. They added muscle as well as money. The building became more attractive. A desperately needed daycare ministry was started. The church continued to send hope into hurting lives and added helping hands to many in desperate need.

Stephen was studying to become a pastor when Sudhakar said yes to God's call. Sudhakar followed Stephen to Bible school and both were enriched by it. After graduating a year apart, the Lord placed each man in churches quite far apart. Both had taken wives and had started their families. At that point, God sharpened Stephen's vision of whom the "them" were in his original call. They were the slum dwellers of the city; the lowest of the low in Indian society. Stephen's immediate response was to challenge his church to start praying for God's leadership as to where they could start a church in one of the nearby slums. The answer surprised them; not only the "where" but also the "what."

Stephen's slum was located in the southern sector of Mumbai in an area called Ambarnath, about a half-hour away from Stephen's church. The location placed it perilously close to the edge of a wadi, a channel where flashfloods, especially from the monsoon rains, ripped every-thing away and flushed it downstream and then out into the ocean. The land was considered too dangerous to put permanent buildings, so a sizeable slum had metastasized there. "Saint" Stephen (he laughed at such foolishness) could not have been more excited to get started there.

Slums are places where Satan has cracked open the earth and let the ooze of hell bubble up. The conditions are semi-organized attempts to manage putrefaction, controlled by the slumlord. And lord he was! There are no laws in the slums, save one: "Obey the slumlord and his muscle." Politicians never went into the slums. Police entered only in groups and that was usually to handle murder victims that weren't caused by the slumlord. The shanties, elbowed into any space available, were made of wood, tin, and unmortared brick, with a roof of canvas or plastic. Most of these structures were about chest high, making it impossible to stand up in them. There were no floors, only dirt (or mud in the rainy season); almost no electricity; nor any bathrooms. Bathroom needs were taken care of in the putrid canal which became a slow moving mass of disease ready to attack anyone it touched. In the nighttime women and girls eliminated just outside the flap of their hovel, otherwise they risked being violated if they went to the canal. Dysentery claimed babies and old people almost daily, like a buzzard that claws and rips roadkill. Stephen knew all that, but he also knew the power of God. He figured that there was no place on earth that could better spotlight God's nature and power than in a slum. Only a Giant could have had such a grand perspective of God as Stephen had.

One day I asked Stephen why anyone would live in such horrible conditions. He laughed and informed me that each slum had a waiting list as long as your arm of people trying to get in. There were so many people moving out of the rural areas into the cities because of the wretched poverty. Those folks had little to nothing so they ended up on the streets, just trying to survive. There was money in the cities and these families hoped to get enough each day to stay alive one more day. The slums were a substantial step upward for them and became their single goal in life.

Stephen got started. He paid an entrance fee (bribe) to build a temporary wooden shack on precarious ground. If it remained in that spot, the shack would be washed away in the monsoons. He only had a few months, but God blessed him. Stephen's church paid a couple from the congregation to live there and supervise ministry from their home in the slum. They started helping by ministering to kids, so both parents could scavenge for food or work. Stephen arranged for a Christian doctor to come in and do a free clinic. They even organized some efforts to help people more effectively look for work. Some folks "got changed" out of all of these efforts so they began an afternoon worship service in the shack. Changed lives reproduced more changed lives.

Then the rains started coming. The slumlord offered to rent another, safer, lot on which to put the temporary shack. Stephen did not know whether it was because of the good things that came from their ministry, or just because the church could make regular weekly payments for the rent. Either way he was delighted.

After that rainy season, Stephen approached the slumlord with a request for a site for a permanent church building. The slumlord mockingly said, "Sure, you can have the edge of the wadi."

"Praise God!" Stephen shouted, and got down on his knees right in front of the slumlord and repeatedly thanked God for this answer. Then Stephen jumped to his feet and went to work.

Stephen and his helpers moved tons of dirt by hand from one side of the wadi to the other. Men and women filled buckets and carried them to the other side to dump them on that special piece of land given for the church building. They looked like an army of two-legged ants with some carrying the buckets in their hands while others placed them on padded cloths on their heads. Throughout the day there was usually some activity, but in the early evening things got much busier as both men and women came home from work and went straight to the wadi. Church members from Stephen's church, together with new believers from the new "shack church" toiled into hard darkness. Even non-Christian slum dwellers participated in this effort. Weeks became months before the foundation was finished at one-and-a-half meters, about five feet.

After a solid foundation firmed up, the people built an attractive, small church building on that foundation. They built it out of block and brick. They fastened a tin roof on it and opened it for the Lord's business. The floors looked like polished, dark tile but were, in fact, hardened and processed cow manure. They literally gleamed. Stephen was able to acquire the aid of a Christian engineer who helped them construct a formidable wedge, made from steel and concrete, to divert the rushing waters during the monsoon season. Then they laid a land bridge from the church to the edge of the wadi with drainage pipes inserted in it. It was a miracle! No two ways about it, this new church building boomingly announced there was a miracle-working God. It also spoke to each heart something just as amazing. People crossed deep divides in the Indian society of ethnicity, economic status, education, wealth, and even caste to work together to build this church building. That was also miraculous. But the neatest part of this miracle was that, because the slumlord gave this land to the church, it fell under his protective sphere; therefore, no one would attack it or try to destroy it. Hallelujah!

How was the miracle of this church building accomplished? A small convention of Baptist churches made a healthy contribution. Stephen's church added some more money. A few successful Christian businessmen gave some offerings. Stephen's own family helped. A few of us on the LEAD team gave anonymous gifts. Even the slum dwellers added a little money, but mostly provided willing backs and hands that made it a reality. Honestly, it took a "Giant of Faith" who knew what God could do through getting people changed, and a commitment to show them God's love. In reality, it took a saint; God's kind, not man's.

GETTING THERE

Getting to Mumbai is as slick as a waterslide at the local theme park. You can fly directly to Mumbai from most of the larger cities in India or even throughout South Asia. Moving from airport to airport is a snap. However, getting from the airport to your destination in the cities constitutes a major hassle. There is a police presence in each baggage claim area because of the frequent squabbles and fights that break out between the porters. You have to be very vigilant and clear as you bargain for each bag to be carried to a car or taxi. Different airports have different expectations concerning the fees that the porters demanded.

After you get to the taxi, the verbal tug of war reaches a new level. You have to know the going rates for each part of the city of your destinations. Being uninformed insures that you pay two to three times the actual fare. Of course, the taxi driver wants to use his meter, if he has one. That is a disaster, as they play with their meters like a concert pianist plays his instrument. Once agreeing on the fare, off you go. The trip adds to your already high blood pressure as the driver constantly blows his horn, hits his brakes (or more likely, pumps his brakes), and screams at everyone who dares get in front of him. When you think it is all over, because you have arrived at the hotel, the driver cranks up the demand for more money than had been agreed upon. At such times, my jagged nerves produce an explosive amount of steam pressuring my anger to spew out over everyone around me. Just before I become the epitome of the "Ugly American," the Holy Spirit reminds me of something very important. Often He uses my sweet wife's gently placed hand on my arm to get my attention to His Word. The Spirit then says, "Remember, you may be the only 'gospel' this driver will ever encounter." At such times, I swallow down some bitter words, smile and hand the driver the amount of money on which we had agreed. Then I add a tip and thank him for getting us safely to the hotel. That's what I did sometimes, but unfortunately, not every time.

On one occasion, Pastor Stephen invited us to a special worship service in the Ambarnath Baptist Church, the one he had planted in the slum. His brother, Sudhakar, met us at our hotel and escorted us across the breadth of Mumbai to the train depot. Trains scoot back and forth across Mumbai like subways in some of the larger cities in the West. The crush of humanity in India is only exacerbated on these trains. We were shocked.

First, we were initiated on what to expect during the auto-rickshaw ride over to the train depot. Three of us were pressed into the seating area designed for two smaller Indian bodies. Literally, our bones were in intimate conversation with each other. The driver almost had to unstick one of us so that we could exit the vehicle. Then the fun began.

The depot was a massive beehive. We could not walk, but had to slip and slide right and left between bodies to go forward, and were in constant contact with others as we moved. I had no idea how Sudhakar knew where to buy our tickets, but he got them. We had been informed that Barbara needed to ride in the Women Only car to prevent from being pinched and fondled. Our cars were right next to each other so that wasn't a problem. Sudhakar got her organized and situated to board the train when it arrived and opened its doors. Then we moved over to our car and got ready. Upon arrival of our train, the people surged toward the door like a swarm of bees headed to their beehive. It was uncanny, like a human magnet had drawn the mass of bodies all at one time. My feet shuffled forward in half steps. There was no control. It was impossible not to go forward. Sudhakar had warned me about stepping up into the train car. You only got one chance. He said some people who had missed the steps had their legs broken because of the panicky surge of those in the back trying to make the train. We made the step and were immediately pressed toward the back of the car. No seats, no benches; it was standing room only. I was carrying my Bible close to my chest as we got sardined in. I dropped my hand to my side but the Bible stayed pressed onto my chest. We lurched away and travelled for an hour and fifteen minutes, all within the city of Mumbai. It was thirty-eight minutes pressed in that mass of humanity before my Bible slipped off my chest and I caught it with my hands.

Sweat dripped off my nose and earlobes, only to fall to my clothes and my neighbor's head. Every part of my lower body was pressed into someone else's body. The smells attacked my nostrils. Not everyone had used Dial soap that morning. Some breaths radiated habits that I strongly rejected. That was the closest thing that I'd ever experienced to being in a straightjacket. I could not move anything. I couldn't scratch my nose, wipe sweat out of my eyes, or change my standing position. It was pure misery.

After about forty-five minutes, enough passengers had exited that we could actually turn around and become unhitched from those around us. I was ever thankful for Sudhakar's instruction about Barbara riding in the Women Only car, which was not as packed as ours.

When we returned later that evening, it was a completely different experience. We all could ride in one car which had a bench. We traversed the huge megacity basically in solitude. No doubt about it, the trip was difficult, but was well worth it in order to be with Giants like Stephen and Sudhakar and experience the "miracle church" in the slum.

BEING THERE

When we went to teach a LEAD seminar in Mumbai it was always with a jingle in our hearts. One of the reasons for that jingle was the

Tungga Paradise Hotel. Not only did the hotel have wonderful clean amenities, good food, and AC, but they had the choicest thing of all, internet access. We actually connected so that we could send and receive emails. What a joy that was. Normally we had to search out an internet café and endure the torturously slow connections with many breaks interrupting our efforts to send and receive precious news from home. Truly the Tungga was a kind of paradise.

Another reason for the jingle was the sweet curd shop about two blocks from the hotel. Sweet curd, a dairy product, has the consistency of a rich, creamy pudding. It starts out tasting velvety sweet and then each bite ends with a sour twang. It is so good. Actually, sweet curd should be sold in a pharmacy and regulated as an addictive drug.

One of the more sobering experiences of all of our treks through India resulted from our walks down to the sweet curd shop. Each time we would pass by Bai (Brother) Rao's "home." Rao was not his real name; I never did find out his name as I never actually met him, so I picked "Rao" for him and his family. You see, Bai Rao's home was a piece of canvas stretched across a cracked and uneven section of sidewalk not far from our hotel. The canvas was fastened to what had been an ornate iron bar extending upward out of a cement wall which enclosed a very old bank building. The Raos had squatter's rights on that same section of sidewalk, night after night. We saw this family multiple times over the years that we taught LEAD seminars in Mumbai. The grandparents got older, much older. The parents became more bent, imitating a question mark. The children grew. There were two grandparents, two parents, and three children. They were ghosts in the daylight that materialized every evening. The dad was a pedicab driver, working long hard and hot days, earning just enough to feed the Rao family a couple of rice and vegetable meals a day. The days he was sick or during the heaviest monsoon rains, I suspect the Raos did not eat. They took baths two blocks away during the evening between five and six o'clock when the city opened certain fire hydrants so those living on the streets could have a bath. People lined up for a block or two, hunched down in a squatting position with a dipper and bar of soap waiting for the line to move a step at time. When one exited the water, another slipped into his position. All were clothed in thin sarongs. Almost all were very thin and none needed to count calories.

After bath time came supper. Mom would cook the rice and vegetables, gleaned that day, in an old paint can. She had a couple of big rocks that she used to balance the can on the edge of the curb. They gathered enough wood every day for the cooking fire. It was a meager meal and barely life-sustaining. I suspect their greatest goal in life was that Mom or Dad could get a small, regular paying job so that they could move into a "real" house in one of the slums.

One of the last times we saw the Raos, I caught the eye of Grandpa Rao. We smiled at each other. He nodded his appreciation of my caring, nonjudgmental look, and I nodded back my deep respect for his taking care of his family in the best way he could. We parted as friends, having never met.

When Barbara and I got back to our "luxurious" room, we looked at the photos of our kids that were always placed somewhere in the room. It made it our home for that time. We looked into the eyes of our kids and just wept. We sobbed for Rao and his precious family and for the uncountable number of Raos in India, in Asia…in the world. Then we cried out loud, in deep appreciation for the lavish blessings our Lord God gives to us and to our loving family each day. At that time, we just looked up and thanked God for the privilege of walking with Giants like Stephen and Sudhakar who obeyed God's call to show His love and power to the lowest of the low in slums like Ambarnath.

14

A LEADER'S GIANT

Pak (Mr.) Abu was a leader of men all of his life. We first met him in Pekanbaru, Indonesia, where we conducted LEAD seminars for pastors and primary church leaders. Pak Abu was not only the most senior participant in age, but also in respect. Young men, barely twenty years old, along with a number of successful pastors in their mid-forties, looked to him for guidance, both in class and out. He was not physically outstanding, at five-feet, eight-inches tall and weighing maybe one hundred-fifty pounds. His cue-ball baldness literally shined and his forehead sloped forward. But it was Pak Abu's eyes that got your immediate attention. They could lock you down in a millisecond, or cause your heart to skip a beat. They also could dance with amusement. Abu started his smile with his eyes that immediately leaped onto his lips and finally spilled all over his sunbaked face. His smiles were always infectious. They invaded the faces of all those who surrounded him.

Pak Abu was born Daniel Abunawar Baurekso in West Java on March 2, 1947. Farming ran red through his arteries. As a small boy, Abu learned the value of hard work. His hands had been chiseled by laboring long hours in the hot sun. They were broad, hard, and calloused. At the same time, Abu's agile mind was sparked alive in school. His voracious appetite for learning came early as he was a quick study on how to read. By high school Abu's intellectual palate jumped from philosophy to religion to science. However high his mind soared, the dirt under his fingernails continued to demand his loyalty to the ground as a farmer.

When Abunawar was eighteen years old, the ever-grasping Communist Party of Indonesia tried to seize power by attempting a military coup. On September 30, 1965, they tried to yank the reins of the nation's leadership into their own exclusive hands by killing five of the six leading generals. Major General Suharto, who had distinguished himself in combat, both against the Japanese and the Dutch, escaped being assassinated on that ill-fated evening. In the following days, Suharto rallied loyal Indonesian members of the armed forces and finally crushed the failed coup attempt. With the military loyal to him, General Suharto gingerly led the infant nation of Indonesia through its darkest hours. For months after the attempted coup, night by night, tens of thousands of local neighbors brutally killed other neighbors who previously had any connection, whatsoever, to the failed Communist Party. An estimated eight hundred thousand to one million Indonesians were slaughtered through those nights of terror. Pak Abu lived through each one of them. He never spoke a word about that time in his life but rumors abounded about how that eighteen-year-old boy became an uncompromising man of steel through some fiery experiences of that nightmarish time. One deep look into Pak Abu's piercing eyes made a quick believer out of me.

The younger Mr. Abu was a portrait of restlessness. He left Java to go to Kalimantan (formerly Borneo) in a program where the government lured citizens from the armpit-crowded island of Java to virgin jungles in Sumatra and Kalimantan by giving them lots of free land. The only catch was it was uncleared jungle. Of course, these transmigrants had the back-breaking work of clearing the land enough to grow crops. Pak Abu was so successful at it that, when he was only thirty years old, President Suharto gave him "The National Farmer Award" for South Kalimantan. After a couple more flip-flops from Java to Sumatra, Abu found God in the center of his piercing eyes. Pak Abu was called from being a farmer to be a "shepherd"; that is, a pastor. He immediately left his farm in central Sumatra and went to the Asian School of Theology in Indonesia, located in Malang, Java. After his graduation three years later, Abu returned to Central Sumatra where he made his home on a government-owned palm oil plantation.

Abu could spell the word sacrifice, both with his mind and body. He had previously cleared his land by his own hands and strength. He worked fourteen- to sixteen-hour days to do so. At that time he regularly ate only ubi, a root kin to our sweet potato, only not so nearly as tasty. Farmers generally used ubi as a belly-filler for pigs or cows. Abu ate it day after day and only added a handful of rice as a reward for attaining certain goals. He stayed the course (like in most challenges in his life) and finally created a substantially profitable farm.

Pak Abu met his wife, Kris, while escorting one of his disciples back to his alma mater in Malang, Java. At age forty-four, he married the love of his life. They lived and loved for the next twenty-four years and God used them both to change hordes of common, hard-working people into God-honoring Christians.

It was missionary Steve Sanders who drew Pak Abu's heart to become a Baptist and start planting Baptist churches all over their palm oil plantation. Steve and his wife, Joy, are the epitome of what being a missionary looks and acts like. Their fingerprints (and boot prints) cover a huge swath of Central Sumatra, where some of the most fierce-hearted followers of Islam have been imbedded for centuries. There will be hundreds (probably thousands) of these Sumatrans in heaven who have called Isa (Jesus), "My Lord and my Savior," because of Steve and Joy. Pak Abu was just one of many that Steve shaped into the man God could use most effectively.

Pak Abu was God's man whether trimming dead palm branches from trees in his grove, or standing behind the handmade pulpit in his living room as he preached to the Baptist congregation that met in his house. The church outgrew Abu's and Kris' home. They literally pushed walls back and sometimes away as the church filled up the porch and overflowed into the front yard. As God's man he always spoke truth, a rare commodity in his environment. Again, it mattered not whether Abu spoke about the price of palm oil, or about the price Jesus paid for your soul, he was believed.

Pastor Abu had planted a solid church in his home. He had won and baptized the majority of his church members. Many had come from an Islamic background, but under Abu's astute leadership, they embraced Jesus as Savior. After establishing this church, he opened two other mission churches. Abu mentored leadership for all three. He sent a few of these young men back to Java for additional theological training, but for the most part, he trained them himself. Most of these he also brought to the LEAD seminars. In the final two years of the LEAD seminars in Pekanbaru before we retired, Abu had baptized seventy-three in one of these mission churches, ninety-six in the other, while another twenty were baptized in his home church.

One day, in a LEAD class, Pak Abu fleshed out who he really was. We used dramas a lot to illustrate biblical truths. On this occasion I had two of the younger men, one from Abu's group, pretend to get into an argument. I was teaching a course on "Christian Lifestyle." They had been planted with no one else knowing about their role play. During the teaching session I opened it up for discussion and, as agreed, they began their charade. Most of the class laughed, at first. The guys started getting louder and more aggressive. Just as their voices became more intense, and I was about to step in to make my point, something even more dramatic happened.

Pak Abu spoke a guttural, explosive command: "Diamlah!" Translated, it could mean, "Be quiet," but in this instance it meant, "Shut up. Not another word!" Abu's eyes could have pierced steel. His face and body language clearly said, "You don't want what happens next if you don't comply." One of the young men looked utterly stunned. The other looked at me in a plea for help. Before I could explain, Abu eased back into his chair and winked at me. He got that mischievous grin on his face that said he saw through us but it had gone too far. Some of the ladies were being frightened. We all exploded in the laughter of relief. But in an instant I knew that I was in the presence of a real man, God's man, and that he had a lot to teach us all. What a Giant Pak Abu was.

GETTING THERE

Disclaimer: The section on "Getting There" is usually a description about the travel challenges of getting to the places where LEAD seminars were taught. However, since we lived in Pekanbaru, Sumatra, our travel challenge for that LEAD seminar was negotiating regular traffic in a modern Indonesian city where there were lined lanes and traffic lights, both of which were obeyed some of the time. It was not difficult. But getting to Pak Abu's house for one of their many Christmas worship services was indeed not only difficult but nearly impossible.

I left Pekanbaru after breakfast to go to Pak Abu's house on the plantation where I had been invited to preach. The service was planned for 7 p.m., which meant it might get started by 7:45 or 8 p.m. No sweat; I gave myself plenty of time so I'd be there early. The trip on the paved roads normally took about three hours. Even though it was December, which meant we were in the heaviest part of the rainy season, my four-wheeled jeep would easily get to the plantation area.

I neared the church member's house, who was also an important official of the palm oil plantation, who lived a few kilometers off of the paved highway. He lived on the main dirt road that ran through the heart of the plantation. I noticed a spider web of smaller tributaries spawned out into the canopied palm groves. These smaller dirt roads, sometimes only two-rutted lanes, connected huge communities of individually-owned palm tree farms. All of these communities had to be connected so that trucks or tractor-pulled wagons could haul off the harvested pods full of palm oil. Each farmer and community had to get their harvested product to the processing factory. It was a massive challenge when all of the dirt roads became, for all practical purposes, flowing, brown, slushy little rivers.

As planned, I was greeted by Mr. Yono, Pak Abu's church member, and four stout young men. Two of them were mentored by Pak Abu while the other two were "muscle" to help us out of hard places, considering the weather. Immediately all five advised that we cancel the trip to Abu's place because of the intensity of the rainy conditions. Of course, there was no phone contact so I could not have informed Pak Abu of a change in plans. I pushed that we should at least try to get there.

Right after an early lunch, off we splashed. One of the young men drove my four-wheeled drive jeep. We went slipping and sliding through the brown slush of the main road, with mud splattering on all of the side windows. There were noticeably no other vehicles on the road. I overheard something from the back seat about, "a foolish American" or worse, as I didn't fully understand the dialect. There were no street or road signs. When we turned off the main highway, the conditions worsened significantly. The road looked like a small river with clumps of grass sticking up out of it. The rain cascaded down in wind-whipped swirls looking like revolving grey sheets. It was nearly impossible to see more than a few feet ahead of us at a time. The driver was good; no, he was fantastic. We negotiated muddy bogs where large trucks had wallowed out deep depressions in the roads. He had the jeep in "ol' granny" (four-wheel drive) and we bobbed onward.

We made a number of detours because of huge washouts. As the greys of the sky darkened, we became aware that the afternoon was slipping and sliding away also. But I could tell from the chatter in the backseat that we were definitely getting closer and, "surprise, surprise'" might even make it. Then it happened.

Suddenly, the front of our jeep dropped its nose precipitously downward and we began to slide forward into a huge bog. With all four wheels whirling in reverse, the jeep slowing sank down into the brown, yucky glue at the bottom of the bog. As soon as the jeep halted, watery mud started easing through the bottom of the doors. At that time, because the battery shorted out, the engine spurted into quietness. I grabbed my Bible, my sandals and took off my batik shirt, which was my "preaching shirt," and struggled to get the door open. I stepped out and sank to above my knees. The jeep had settled down in the mud which had surged just over the tops of all four tires. The whole jeep was below the horizon of the road. With the help of two young men, I escaped the mud monster and got back up onto the road. The rain continued to gush out of the sky, with long periods where it fizzled into a mere drizzle. The four guys pointed me down the watery road and said that I'd find Pak Abu's house about two kilometers, a little over one mile, in that direction. They would stay with the jeep and maybe someone would come along and pull it out.

I walked into the yard amongst a crowd that had already begun to arrive. I was some kind of spectacle, looking literally like the walking Mud Man. Pak Abu appeared, looking out from under his umbrella, and essentially said, "You are one crazy man." Then he grinned and added something about having "heart." I bathed in his outside bathroom by the bucket-drawn well. I cleaned off my pants, put my preaching shirt back on, and went into a joyous celebration. As I was finishing my message, my four very muddy young men showed up at the worship service. A large plantation truck, the only other vehicle we saw during the entire trip, had showed up and, with a lot of effort, pulled the sunken jeep out of the bog. The green jeep had been repainted in mud-brown.

After the service, Pak Abu instructed us to leave immediately as the weather was going to get worse, potentially stranding us for two or three days. He sent a guide on his motorcycle through the grove trees, hardly crossing any of the normal roads until we got back to the main road. It was a much shorter trip home. I drove on that night arriving home early in the morning as one dead-tired puppy dog.

That trip was retold for years. It seemed to have given me some added credibility points, as the LEAD participants showed even more appreciation for our teachings. And it also knitted my heart to Pak Abu's in a special way. It allowed me to be close to a man that I greatly admired, a true Giant of the faith.

BEING THERE

"Being there" in Pekanbaru meant sleeping in our own bed, studying at our own desks and freely doing emails. We lived at home and travelled back and forth to the Riau Training Center. This training center was under Steve Sanders' ministry and was the Cadillac of all the LEAD seminar facilities. The participants loved it because the" RTC" was modern, in a city with a lot of goodies that weren't available where most of them lived and ministered, plus the food was top-notch. There was one other thing—the Durian Fest. During every LEAD seminar, Steve would host all the participants at a local Baptist orphanage where they would eat all the durian that they desired. The orphanage was on the edge of the city and the kids and staff loved this event too, because it meant they got to eat all of the durian they wanted. A win-win situation, plus the kids cleaned up all of the mess. Steve would haul in a pickup truck full of durians that he bought from a local durian farmer.

Durian! The sound of the word immediately brings two reactions to those who have encountered this exotic Asian fruit. One reaction is to go cross-eyed in pure ecstasy over its heavenly taste. The other reaction people have is grabbing your mouth on the way to the toilet where you are sure there will be a stomach eruption. People either love durian or hate it. There are no fence-sitters. My best description is if you took hundreds of eggs, let them rot in the boiling sun, and then dropped them into a septic tank with its rancid contents, you would have a start to the smell of durian. Then put all the yuck from a pigsty and all of the rank, smelly droppings of the chicken yard into the same tank. Close the septic tank and bake that rancid concoction for thirty cloudless days. On the thirty-first day, yank off the top of that septic tank so that the explosive, putrid odor leaps out and assaults your nose, then you would understand the smell of one small durian when whacked open by a machete. To quote one small child from the orphanage, "Ugh, it stinks bad." It really does. That's why you can be fined in Singapore for carrying a durian onto public vehicles or into a hotel.

But the taste is described by those who overcome their first nauseous feelings and actually put some of the inner fruit into their mouths as, "Heaven descending and resting on their tongues." For durian lovers, that off-white, yellowish glob of succulent, heavenly fruit brings satisfaction to the palate that almost nothing else can match. From those surrounding the durian filled pickup truck came sounds like, "Ahh, best ever; sooooo good. One more piece, please." Truly it was a fest and a feast, with juices running down the faces and off of the elbows.

We will carry that picture in our hearts for the rest of our lives. Two Giants, grinning, juices running off of their elbows while sharing a durian. These two shared much more. Both Steve and Pak Abu shared a vision of reaching fierce-hearted people with the gospel, winning them to Jesus Christ and starting churches among them. These two were Giants—God's men for God's job.

15

THE MUSTARD-SEED GIANT

Nazir Masih was the pastor of the Chandigarh Baptist Church in Northern India, where we held one of our LEAD seminars. He met us on the platform at the Chandigarh train depot. On that day, Pastor Nazir was totally animated. His eyes twinkled, his hands punctuated the air like a tent evangelist, and his broken English fired in a staccato manner sounding a lot like a machine gun.

"Come, come, we mus' go see da land," Nazir urged while leading us to his older car, a grey Holden. We were swept away without the normal pleasantries.

"We've boughta city block for da school," said Nazir while shifting gears and flashing a certificate in the air like a pom-pom at a school's pep rally. Nazir's eyes glistened and his voice tightened as he proclaimed, "We pray to da Got (God) and He gave us…" After a little while we came to understand that when Nazir said "gave" he meant "gave the opportunity to 'buy' a city block" from the city. We knew that the church had been praying about starting a school to reach hundreds of families for Christ. They actually had been saving a percentage of their offerings toward buying land for this school for the last few years. Nazir and some of the elders of the church had concluded the negotiations with the city for that block only a few days before we arrived and it was only three blocks from the church building.

We arrived. Pastor Nazir jumped out and proclaimed, as if he were an ancient explorer from past centuries, "Look! The Got's land! We will build a school on it." Truly the land was impressive. The city had restricted the entire block from any buildings being put on it. It was an empty block surrounded by nice houses and multistoried apartment buildings which were well maintained. At that moment, Nazir explained that the church had put down their entire savings of $100,000, which was 20 percent, as a deposit.

We were shocked. "But Brother Nazir," I blurted out, "How are you going to pay the remaining $500,000 for the land and then have anything to build with?"

"Da Got. He knows. He will give us…just like this time," Nazir answered. His smile never wavered. His eyes became expansive mirrors of his deep convictions. Through his eyes we could see large, well-equipped buildings with students flowing in and out; parents beaming their approval as they gathered up their kids; a church building having to expand because of the overflow attendance. Wow! What a vision. It took our breaths away as we saw through the eyes of the Mustard-Seed Giant.

This was not Nazir's first foray into the arena demanding great faith. He had entered the ministry later in life than most. He had been a very successful business man, affording him prime rewards such as a two-story house and a brand new luxury sedan each year. Then, in his mid-forties, God changed gears and called Nazir to pastor the growing Baptist Church of Chandigarh. Nazir quickly responded by selling his house and moving his charming wife and kids to Chandigarh to become a pastor. Such a move in any country would be challenging, but in India, that transition could be considered nearly miraculous. The giant leap downward, financially, was handled with grace and humility by Nazir and his amazing family.

Nazir Masih developed a rare form of church planting after he assumed the role of the pastor. He focused on developing spiritual leaders, especially biblically founded deacons. He was not jealous or power-hungry. Nazir shared opportunities to serve with his deacons, both spiritually and organizationally. This was a fairly unique perspective among Indian pastors.

The church began to grow and the sanctuary became packed. Pastor Nazir, with other church leaders, broke off fifty to sixty church members with two deacons and sent them out to form a church in one of the sections of Chandigarh that had little Christian witness. From then on, each time the sanctuary became full again, they commissioned a group of church members, along with two deacons to function as pastors, and sent them to another part of the city.

On each occasion that a group was splintered off to a different part of the city, the Mother Church rented a building for the group, bought supplies and paid a pastor's honorarium for one month. After one month, the new church was self-supporting. According to Nazir, "They are 'church' before the move so they are still 'church' after the move. They don't need 'to become' church; they already are. They give tithe now. They give tithe then. Deacon lead here. Deacon lead there. All 'same-same'; no difference."

After ten years of this kind of church planting, Nazir had led the Chandigarh Baptist Church to plant seven new, thriving churches. The combined baptisms, of those won to Christ in the Mother Church, and all of these new churches, totaled ten thousand new believers. Each of these churches continued with over half of them building new buildings. Only a Giant with vision and great faith could have accomplished those results.

At the same time Pastor Nazir was shining the gospel light into the darker sections of his city, he also trained bright searchlights into the vast regions west of Chandigarh called the Punjab. The Punjab was hazardous to human health and demanded resolute constitutions to survive in it, much less to try to plant churches. Nazir's vision required sturdy men and women carrying the gospel into this difficult area so he led his church in sending men and some couples to the Punjab, as God provided them. After a few years, the Chandigarh Baptist Church was supporting fifteen to twenty-five church planters in the Punjab. These men and women made up the larger percentage of our LEAD seminars held in Chandigarh. After studying Personal Evangelism and Church Planting in one seminar, these church planters went out and planted 105 churches in the following six months. Not all of those churches survived, although most did.

One of the church planters, Pastor Salim Masih recounted, "We started going to the poorer people and asked them if they wanted us to pray for healing either for diseases or demons. Many agreed and countless healings occurred and legions of demons were chased out. It was like the New Testament days." Many of these Punjabis grew into strong Christians and established strong churches. Hope sprung forth and many caught the vision that had started in the soul of the Mustard-Seed Giant, Nazir Masih.

Within three years the city block was paid off and small buildings were erected to start the school. The Mother Church continued to divide and conquer. The Punjab saw real rays of "Sonshine." All of this was because Nazir Masih left the business world to do God's business. Nazir possessed an amazing faith in "Da Got who could…" Nazir's great faith was infectious. You could not be around the man without having your own faith expanded. We were always changed for the better by each meeting we had with the Mustard-Seed Giant.

GETTING THERE

Platforms in Indian train depots were daunting. On them the full strata of life-forms in India seemed to ooze up. We usually had to wait from half an hour to three hours for our particular train to appear. That trains actually ran on any semi-organized fashion at all was a modern day miracle. Incidents caused by the typical crush of people in India affected train schedules daily. Trains hit people who slept on the tracks or were drunk or just too exhausted to move. There were also collisions with animals, pedal-cabs and other vehicles, especially at night. Flashing lights were a waste of electricity in the rural Indian countryside. Then there were times when the water tanks sprang leaks and the train's water supply was met by a human chain of bucket-passers from a local well. Once in a while there was a serious collision of trains that took up to twelve hours to be cleared before the tracks could be used again.

In train depots, our Western white faces always sent out silent invitations to every beggar within a five-mile radius. You could tell where a Westerner was by the group of wretched humanity that surrounded us. Every time, there would be mothers with emaciated infants who were being pinched to make them cry, or in a dulled state appearing as though they were dying. All of these mothers extended their hands and, with pleading eyes motioned for something to eat, for them, or for their babies. At the same time, all of the raggedly clothed two-to-three-year-olds mimicked their mothers. Often all of this was accompanied by moans and pleas for money, in English, of course. Sitting in the midst of such commotion was not for the timid soul.

We had made the rookie mistake earlier by trying to give some money to a poor woman with pathetic-looking kids. It almost caused a riot. We had forgotten the "Asian factor," in that whatever you do for one in a certain situation, you are expected to do for all in that same environment. So we learned to pray for each one in front of us, endure, and sometimes cause a diversion.

At times, I stood up and walked over to a group of children and knelt down saying, "No money. No money." But I asked their names and ages. Someone in the circle would always translate. Being close to the children allowed one of them to reach out and touch my white skin. Invariably, the children overcame their hesitation and rubbed on my exposed arm and ran their fingers across the hairs on my arms. Many times they played with the hair on our arms and just shuddered with glee. To them, it seemed as good as a ride at Disney World. Those were magical moments when all of us became God's creation without distinction of being Western, white or brown, affluent, or poor; we were momentarily heart-linked together and it felt good. It did not last long but was a rare pleasure each time it did happen.

We had negotiated with the porters, so that when the train arrived, they grabbed our two suitcases and carried them to the correct train car and our compartment. We rode Second Class, which meant we shared one compartment with other passengers. It had two long, but comfortable, bench seats which faced each other. It always made for interesting interaction in that we shared some common space, but usually not a common language. After trying to unsuccessfully communicate, we usually settled into smiles and nods as the countryside slipped by scene by scene.

Rural northern India reflects a patchwork of greens and browns. The greens are painted by a water supply. There are a few small, meandering rivers that trickle down into a spider web of creeks that flow above ground only for a part of the year. Some springs also dot the countryside like oases in the desert. All represent life and struggles. Each area of green has an intriguing history of power and deception that rivals anything coming out of the King Arthur period of England, minus the steed and lance. The flickering scenes aptly reflect modern day India in which a relatively few, affluent people squeezed the life out of the laborers, one hot day after another with suffocatingly low wages. All of this is sanctioned by the caste system of Hinduism.

Occasionally on our trip we would see hope framed in the train window in the form of what seemed to be a cow barn converted into a church building. With half-bricked walls, completed by thatched materials that supported tin roofs, each church building had a white cross fixed to its front door. Each of these crosses was empty indicating that Jesus was no longer pinned to His cross but was indeed resurrected and alive. His empty tomb radiated hope to all, the oppressed and the oppressor.

After seven-and-a-half hours, we arrived in Chandigarh. It had been a full day but a good day. After bargaining with porters again, we left the train and found Pastor Nazir waiting for us. He was so exuberant. We knew something big was up. What a shock when we found out that the Chandigarh Baptist Church was buying a city block for the future Baptist School of Chandigarh. What a Giant!

BEING THERE

Chandigarh has a sense of newness like that of opening the doors of a new car. The city was designed and built by Indians after their independence. This new city had been completed in 1962. Chandigarh feels totally different when compared to Mumbai (Bombay) or Kolkata (Calcutta). Those two cities evoke a sense of history long past and of ancient occurrences that happened before pen and paper. That is not the case with Chandigarh. There are no crumbling buildings that reflect a past century's architecture. The streets are straight and relatively clean. There is a decipherable appreciation and pride toward progressiveness among the inhabitants of Chandigarh as they seem more focused on getting ahead instead of battening down the hatches for mere survival.

We loved going to Chandigarh, except in April. In April the temperatures topped out every day around 110-degrees Fahrenheit. The air seemed to attack you with a hot pitchfork! When we walked on the sidewalk, heat rays radiated upward, chasing away the oxygen from our noses. Sometimes, it really was hard to breathe. Since we took opened pedicabs to and from the seminar site, we experienced an oven-blast of sizzling hot air for the entire trip, which caused more discomfort than relief.

The hotel of choice for LEAD teachers while in Chandigarh was the Park Hotel, which was only a few blocks from where we conducted the seminars. We chose the Park Hotel because, when requested, they would not turn off the AC compressor during the early morning hours in order to save money. When they did turn the compressors off, the fans were left blowing, which did little to cool. In those times, we woke up on damp pillows and sheets. Each time in April, upon checking in, we requested a meeting with the manager on duty and stated that we expected twenty-four-hour AC for what we paid. He always smiled and wagged his head in good Indian fashion assuring us that we would be comfortable.

Now, three years after the church had purchased the city block, they had paid off their debt and had constructed two single-story concrete block buildings where they had begun their school. After another year, they built a multistoried building for the school and the concrete buildings became storage units. While they were working on the real school building, we used the block buildings for the LEAD seminars. In April, these cubicles, with ceilings only seven-feet high topped by a tin roof, became saunas. Nazir could have inexpensively opened a spa in these two buildings since the steam was produced naturally. We taught six-and-a-half hours a day in one of these saunas and our clothes would be drenched as though we had fallen into a swimming pool. We had to wash out the salt stains each night because of the amount of sweat we poured into them each day. Most afternoons, after teaching all day, we came home and took a long, cold shower. On those days, we often took two showers a day. The hotel saved money on us because we rarely used any hot water. Day by day, we were wrung out as our energies were squeezed out of our pores. By the end of the week we felt like the proverbial wet noodle. Chandigarh, in April, was always challenging.

The participants, however, made every hour worthwhile. Nazir selected trustworthy men and couples. These valiant souls rode on top of buses and in the cattle-car section of the trains where there were no seats, but plenty of goats and chicken coops. These were unpretentious souls, down to earth, able to survive in any environment. These church planters were constantly on the move, both for safety reasons, and in order to be productive in their ministry.

We loved teaching these folks in Chandigarh. Most of their questions started with, "How," not with "Why." These good servants of God constantly pushed us to tell them how to teach, how to behave, how to win lost souls to Christ; they always focused on application. Often, they would say toward the end of the week: "Brother Harry, Sister Barbara, this is all we ever get, so be sure to give us all you've got." And we did! We gave all because we knew we were privileged to be with some of God's finest when we were in Chandigarh. It was one of our chief joys and great privileges to be with those precious souls, soggy clothes and all.

16

THE TURNCOAT
WHO TURNS HEARTS

Saleem (not his real name) grew up in a strict Muslim home in northern Bangladesh. From his family's example, Saleem adopted disdain for Christians and Hindus. Because they were resistant infidels, organized to oppose all that the prophet Mohammed taught, Saleem justifiably hated both religions and their blind followers.

Then in high school, Saleem met one of these infidels up close and personal. Onto was a Christian inside and out. He had an answer for the constant attacks on his character and beliefs. Even when the hotheads bloodied him up, Onto seemingly left his anger on the dirty floor or in the bloody sink where he cleaned himself. But Onto would never cower down on any insult or assault. He kept on taking the next step forward. In fact, as Saleem remembered, "Onto was pretty impressive."

Remarkably, Saleem and Onto became friends. Saleem learned a great deal about Jesus, whom he knew as the prophet Isa, and was gradually attracted to Him. About halfway through Saleem's second year in high school, his life was thrown into total chaos. This turmoil was precipitated by an invitation from a white man to share a pedicab ride. Saleem's school was quite far from his home, so on that particularly hot day, he accepted the invite to ride instead of hoofing it. Shockingly, that white man spoke "Bangla" (Bengali). What Saleem did not realize was that this white man was a missionary who used this technique to witness to as many as would accept it. The man explained who Jesus was and that He came to earth to die for our sins and was resurrected three days after His crucifixion. Through this process, the man shared that hearts were made clean and acceptable to God for everyone who accepted Jesus as their only God and Savior.

Saleem was shocked as if lightning had hit him. It was like a murky cloth had been lifted from his spiritual eyes. All he now knew about Isa paved the way in understanding who Jesus was and in following Him. That evening at his bedside, Saleem made the decision that changed his life, both then and for eternity.

A short while later Saleem revealed to his family his decision to become a follower of Jesus. They tried to get him to "quit such foolishness," but Saleem did not budge. His family threatened him and finally removed him, not only from their home but from their hearts as well. They declared him dead. He had lost everything—his home, his family, and his support in life. At that moment Onto's family took him in and gave him a place to live, at least until he finished high school. God used that time to build in Saleem's life a deep foundation on God's Word.

It turned out that Saleem was a gifted businessman. He saw opportunities and could make deals that others missed altogether. Profits mounted up gradually and within a few years he had become very successful. Then God said to him, "OK, son, it's time now." Saleem had used a certain model to expand his businesses and he began to use the same model to grow "God's business." Not long afterwards, "franchises" (house churches) began popping up everywhere but especially in strong Muslim neighborhoods. Saleem called his franchise leaders, "Chairmen and Supervisors." Saleem's model was clearly a business model but God blessed it.

One day Barbara and I met with Saleem. He poured his heart out. He desperately needed leaders; pastors, teachers, and franchise-planters better equipped to lead these growing groups. LEAD was one of God's answers to Saleem's problem. The challenge was to train those willing leaders close to where they lived without putting a bright spotlight on it as Christian training.

There was one incident that typified how God worked to meet Saleem's need. We were in the third session of training Saleem's leaders in one neighborhood, meeting in an older house on the edge of town rented by one of Saleem's businesses. Because of the potential danger being in such a religiously volatile region, our instructions had been very clear. We were not to go out of that house until the following Friday evening when we'd be picked up after dark and returned to Dhaka, the capital city. Everything done that week was hush-hush. We sang in whispers and clapped with our fingertips.

The men and three women were a delight to teach. We simplified the materials to the bare basics and repeated them over again. We used games, small group work, and dramas to illustrate the truths of God's Word. On about Thursday of that week a knock came on the front door. Suddenly, we all became petrified. We envisioned the Muslim-controlled police at the door ready to raid us. Saleem's coordinator answered the door. Two women stood there. One started pleading to be baptized. They were quickly ushered into the house. Both ladies were from that community. One had received Christ earlier at the "franchise" that met in the house we were using and had been baptized in a water tank used for splash baths. Her life had changed so radically that her friend saw it and wanted what she had, and she wanted it immediately. The coordinator led her to Christ and promised to baptize her the following Friday evening after the worship service.

Some things you cannot hide with a closed door, like a dramatically changed life. So we finished our teaching on Friday morning and left after dark that same evening just before the worship service and baptism. For our safety and theirs, we had to leave. But God had not left. Nor had the effect of His Word in the hearts of Saleem's courageous leaders. For some, Saleem, a gentle Giant of the faith, was a "turncoat," but for others he was God's instrument, turning a mass of hearts to the Lord Jesus.

GETTING THERE

Getting from Bangalore, India, to Dhaka, Bangladesh, is as simple as one, two, three. We would fly from Bangalore to Calcutta, India, and then on over to Dhaka. But the Lord has a sense of humor sometimes, like the previous trip we had made to Dhaka about a year before.

As usual, we had reconfirmed our tickets and selected our seats for the trip to Dhaka. We had arrived two hours in advance of the flight time, which was normal for us, only to discover there was no scheduled flight to Dhaka at that time for that day. There had been one when we booked the flight, but it had been cancelled two months prior to that day at the airport. We showed them our valid tickets which had been sold to us about one month previously. That was one month after the official cancellation of that particular flight. We even gave them the confirmation number and seat assignments given to us only two weeks before the expected flight. This had all been done at their downtown office in Bangalore. Unbelievable! However, what became truly unbelievable was the responsible way the Indian Airline agent at the airport responded. He admitted it was the airline's fault and promised to get us to Dhaka that day, whatever it took. He rescheduled us to go far northwest to Delhi and then catch a direct flight from Delhi to Dhaka. We flew a thousand miles out of our way which added a few hours, but it would get us to Dhaka. Perfect. The only problem was that when we checked in at the Delhi airport for our connection to Dhaka, for some unexplainable reason, the flight had already left one-and-a-half hours earlier than scheduled. Therefore, after a five-hour layover, we caught a second flight to Dhaka. Finally we boarded that second flight to Dhaka having already logged more than twelve hours in the trip. Oops. After a half hour, we were told we'd have to deplane as there was some crucial repair needed to be made before we could depart to Dhaka. We finally got into Dhaka that night about midnight. The normal four-hour trip had taken fifteen hours…all in a day's work while travelling in South Asia.

However, this time was one, two, three, and we were in Dhaka within four hours as scheduled. Praise the Lord.

BEING THERE

One of the opportunities for service by the LEAD team, while serving in Bangladesh, was to teach some of the emerging leaders from the tribal groups located in south Bangladesh. These groups were ministered to by a missionary who lived in Chittagong. He made all of the arrangements and was so gracious to get the LEAD team members to the various places where seminars were conducted. It was always a joyful experience when we went to Chittagong, in south Bangladesh, because of the sweet fellowship experienced with this missionary and his family, plus being with the tribal leaders because they needed us so badly.

On one occasion we arrived in Chittagong on October 6, 2001. After a delightful overnight, we left on our arranged transportation to the Dishari Camp which was near the small town of Banshakhali. We had the pleasure of taking Brother Mritunjoy (Mree-tun-joy) with us who was our primary translator and seminar coordinator. The jeep trip took more than two hours, depending on how many vehicles were waiting to get through some of the mud holes that populated the roads every few miles. When a truck or bus became stuck, it took a little longer. Plus, we had to cross the wide Karnaphuli River by ferry boat. That venture, always chaotic, could be made easier depending on how willing you were to add a little more to the ticket price.

The drive was usually very pleasant as the two-lane road, sometimes reduced to one, weaved in and out of small towns and villages along the way. Much of the road was canopied by large trees, limbs embracing over the road. Even though the trip was pleasant enough, we were always glad to get to the camp in order to get organized. We wanted to be settled and prepared before the seminar started.

The guest rooms were spartan, as most camp guestrooms were. We had two bunkbeds in our room. Bunkbeds were always a plus because it allowed us to use the second mattress as extra padding on top of our own. That way, we were kept off the slats underneath the mattresses. There was no shelf space, but the room had a table so we could set up our computer. Fortunately we carried an extension cord with multiple outlets on it as the room only had one electrical outlet. The electricity was intermittent, but when it was on we enjoyed the ceiling fan. Through experience, we had learned to carry a rope which we tied in the bathroom in order to dry our towels after a refreshing splash bath at night. We also kept a handy supply of mosquito coils that we burned each night. The coils were amazingly efficient. They kept the blood suckers off us every night. Batteries were needed to keep our lights and gadgets functioning, so we carried a couple of pounds of various sized batteries wherever we went. Yes, our bags were a bit on the heavy side.

The men and women flocked in before sunset on Sunday, October 7. They had travelled for hours. Many had walked quite a long way before they caught a bus. Often they required two or three transfers before getting to the camp. Some came by boat and then by foot, but almost everyone was ready by 7 p.m. on Sunday evening for the opening ceremony.

At 8 a.m. Monday morning, after a hearty but spicy breakfast, we launched into the first subject. I noticed there was a lot of whispering, shaking of heads, and a slight atmosphere of agitation. This was highly unusual for this group of tribal leaders. Normally they were laser-beam focused on what was being taught. I mentioned this to Brother Mritunjoy, but he sidestepped the issue. The problem grew during the second hour of study.

During the break time, Sajal Mollick told us that U.S. coalition forces had started bombing Afghanistan that morning. The U.S. was responding to the attack on the Twin Towers on September 11, 2001. There were wild numbers of casualties being reported and it was not being received well in this vastly Islamic majority nation. Sajal was clearly nervous. He mentioned that the local Muslims in the market-place were going crazy. He was obviously worried, and so were the tribal leaders, as they were often identified as Christians by the general Muslim population of Bangladesh.

It was at that moment that we received a telephone call confirming everything our brothers and sisters already knew. It was not safe for Americans to be out in public at this time in Bangladesh, and it was especially perilous to be in the more radical rural areas at that time. It was also unsafe for Bangladeshi Christians to be out in the open. In this Christian Retreat Center, fifty miles out in the boonies, we were all targets for reprisals from the agitated Muslims. We had to get out!

Our leadership organized a bus to pick us up right after dark and take us to Chittagong. By that time, Sajal had gotten word that there would be an attack on the retreat center that evening "to rid the earth of those Americans and Christian preachers." We quickly packed and prayed. It was a long afternoon.

We all boarded the bus at dusk with a Christian driver. The tribal leaders decided to put Barbara and me in the middle of the bus, across the aisle from one another. Then, those precious tribal brothers and sisters enclosed us like a blanket. They also decided to keep every window in the bus completely closed. It became a sauna in a split second and remained so for the entire trip. The bus traversed through villages and small towns where mobs of people were out with torches, angrily shouting into the wind. We all knew that if we were discovered they would most likely burn us alive in that bus. For more than two hours, minute by minute, we held our collective breaths. Each time we slowed to a crawl because of people flooding into the roads, our "blanket" wrapped around us even more tightly. These cherished souls, who could not speak five understandable words to us with their mouths, spoke volumes of love for us with their hearts by putting their sweat-dripping bodies between us and harm's way. We were so humbled by their extraordinary concern.

The ferry crossing was knuckle-cracking tense. The waiting, the collective sizzle with sweat dripping on the dirty floor, and the heart-pounding seemed to last forever. But once on the other side of the Karnaphuli River, it was smooth sailing. Some finally cracked their windows and there was an audible sigh of relief. Upon arrival in Chittagong, there was joy abounding and all were ready for a bath and a bed.

One year later, we returned to Dishari Camp and all went well. However, that bus trip had bonded our hearts like a celestial welding. When you face martyrdom together it changes something in the very fiber of your being. That experience melded our hearts and souls together. One day in heaven, where language will not be a problem, we may still be talking with each other about that night. With Saleem in the north and the tribal leaders in the south, we constantly thanked God for the privilege of walking hand-in-hand with both groups as He often did remarkable things in front of our very own eyes in both areas.

17

A Beautiful Man
in a Beautiful Land

Wayne Joseph is not a "beautiful man" by Bollywood (India's Hollywood) standards. Wayne's beauty is not reflected in his face or body, but in his heart and "feet." The prophet Isaiah defined that kind of beauty when he wrote:

"How beautiful upon the mountains are the feet of him who brings good news, who proclaims peace, who brings glad tidings of good things, who proclaims salvation..." (Isaiah 52:7).

Later in the New Testament, the apostle Paul defined the one who brings the "Good News" as one who is "preaching the gospel." As God looked down the corridors of time, He saw a man in the coastal region on the east coast of India who embodied those truths. Wayne Joseph is his name.

When we came to know Wayne, he was splitting his time between the beautiful land of Araku Valley and his home city of Visakhapatnam. Visak, short for Visakhapatnam, is located on the coastline in Central India. It is a three-hour drive between Visak and Araku. The Araku Valley is nestled down between the Eastern Ghats of India, and is always a scenic drive; that is, when you dared to take your eyes off the treacherous and challenging mountain road. The trips reminded us of some windy roads in the Smokey Mountains of North Carolina.

Wayne was born into a family with a heritage of Isaiah's beautiful feet. His father, Victor, had worked with some Canadian Baptists who had targeted the nine tribes, or ethnic groups, in the Araku Valley. Even as an older child and teenager, Wayne had been involved in sharing the gospel. Then something happened that would alter his life forever.

God urged Wayne to go up to the fanatical Hindu state of Bihar and evangelize the people there. Wayne obeyed and went. Knowing that he could not openly share the gospel or preach without immediately being killed, he shared about Jesus over coffee in the small roadside eating places that usually consisted of a few poles and a thatched roof. There were some who were genuinely interested, but most were more interested in his wallet than in his heart.

One day, as he returned to his rented room, he rounded the corner and found a small mob of angry men standing close to his residence. Some of those men brandished machetes, others had long knives with wavy blades, called krises, while others held stout clubs in their hands. Upon seeing Wayne, they erupted into animal-like howls, angry shouts, and threats of death. Wayne turned and bolted down the unpaved street toward some small hills close to the village. The mob of nearly twenty shouting men gave chase, waving their weapons in the air. The scene was reminiscent of the old Western flicks where the American Indians chased after a lone cowboy, whooping and hollering, as they waved their tomahawks in the air. Wayne started up the hill and entered a small grove of trees. He heard his pursuers not far behind him.

And then it happened. He tripped on a raised root and went down, face first, with a thud. He remembered raising his arms to protect the back of his neck and waiting, with eyes closed, for the first crushing blow.

Suddenly, everything went black. According to Wayne, when he became conscious again, he was about twenty kilometers from the spot where he had tripped. He was on the other side of the hill, with his face still pressed into the earth. Wayne offers no explanation as to why he wasn't martyred or how he ended up where he did, other than to quote Jesus:

"I saw Satan fall like lightning from heaven. Behold, I give you authority to trample on serpents and scorpions, and over all the power of the enemy. And nothing shall, by any means, hurt you." (Luke 10:18-19)

After that experience, Wayne was a changed person. He continued to mature in the Lord, and God gave him his wife, Linda, and two children. A few years later, God gave Wayne the opportunity to inherit his father's ministry in the Araku Valley, which Wayne assumed with grace and strength. God expanded Wayne's vision to not just engage all nine tribes in the Araku Valley, but to plant a church in every village. To accomplish this vision, Wayne and Linda continued the ministry of an orphanage for the needy children of that valley. In addition, they also continued to support a number of evangelists and church planters who started churches up and down that beautiful land.

For years afterwards, miracles continued to surround Wayne like moths around a lightbulb at night. The account of Satyanadam's conversion is just one stunning example. Satyanadam was a sadistically cruel criminal. While in prison, he bragged about how many women's hands he had chopped off in order to steal their gold bracelets. During a prison visitation, Wayne confronted him with the gospel and its ultimate power and Satyanadam was miraculously saved and started growing spiritually in prison. When he was released, Wayne helped him receive some Bible training and then he became the pastor of a growing church on "King Jesus Mountain." That was Satyanadam's name for the mountain, not the government's.

Another notable miracle happened after LEAD began to minister in the Araku Valley. Pastor Jason, already an old man in his sixties, had not been allowed to attend school as a child. His childhood years had been tough and survival was more important than education. Even as a child, his arms and back had been needed to provide food for his family's table. He had never learned to read. However, God saved him later in life and called him into His service. Jason, having developed a good memory, had memorized a large number of Bible stories. When God set him as a shepherd of a small mountain church in Araku, Jason basically told those stories and made application, but his heart's desire was to actually read his Bible. Every morning in his devotions, each time he preached, and every time he attended a LEAD seminar, Jason had his Bible open. But more times than not, it was upside down.

Then one day, in early morning devotions, Pastor Jason began to comprehend what all of those squiggly marks meant on the page of his Bible. He could read! His testimony was, "I was given the gift of eyes." After all, if the gift of tongues involved speaking, then the gift of eyes involved reading. Interestingly enough, Pastor Jason could only read the Bible, not a newspaper or even a printed Bible study page; just the Bible. That wasn't a problem for Pastor Jason because the Bible was all he wanted to read, anyway.

It was always a privilege to stand beside Wayne, with his "beautiful feet" in that beautiful land of the Araku Valley. The reason God had hung numerous miracles around his neck bewildered Wayne as much as anyone. He described his feelings each time something extraordinary happened with these words, "Like when I woke up in Bihar, twenty kilometers from where I tripped, I could only think of one explanation: God had something else for me to do." He continued, "So I try to find out what it is and go do it."

What a Giant! What a privilege!

GETTING THERE

Going to the Araku Valley meant flying into Visakhapatnam and overnighting at the Green Star Hotel. What an oasis in the midst of a dry, thorny land was the Green Star Hotel! It had electricity, hot water, and even air conditioning; all of which functioned most of the time. The Green Star also provided a luscious buffet breakfast that became one of the highlights of the entire four-month trek teaching in India. In fact, the Araku Valley experience was considered one of the sugarplums of all the places we taught.

Often on Fridays, after our seminar was completed at noon, we would travel back to Visak, and Wayne and Linda would join us for dinner. The Green Star Hotel's restaurant was one of our favorites among a few others we tried. The food was secondary, though we always enjoyed it. It was the fellowship with these two Giants of the faith that registered the highest on our appreciation scale. We would debrief the seminar and talk about adjustments needed to make them better and more productive. These treasured evenings went far beyond the needs of the Araku Valley. They became the cloak that wrapped our hearts together into one cohesive unit. Through these times, God shaped us into His productive servants; in a city, a valley, and throughout South and Southeast Asia.

After the goodbyes were said, then came the long anticipated bath. We had dreamed of that luxuriating bath for days. Hot water flowing into a real bathtub; a bathtub where one could lie back and "roast" into a warm pink color. It was almost sinful that we enjoyed that particular bath so much. Almost…

On one occasion, early in our trips to the Araku Valley and the return to Green Star Hotel, the water was only tepid for that anticipated bath. I spoke to the duty manager the next morning and received an appropriate apology. Others reported similar experiences. So, the following time we came to the Green Star Hotel, I pressed about why many of us had this same occurrence. At that time an assistant manager took me aside and admitted that they turned the furnace off at 9 p.m. in order to save money. His thinking was since most Indians take their baths early in the morning or in late afternoon, he could not imagine the need for a bath after 9 p.m. We made the adjustment and all was well.

The trip to Araku Valley from Visak went up the eastern side of the Eastern Ghat Mountains and then back down into a beautiful and wide valley. The road was in fairly good shape. However, they did conserve on the tar when it came to the width of that road. After all, it was built on ledges and carved-out sections of the mountain. As we headed toward Araku Valley, it wasn't too bad because we were on the mountain side of the road. India had copied the British regarding which side of the road to drive on, which is the opposite from the United States. Therefore, returning to Visak from Araku Valley put us on the "thrill side" of the road. There would be too many times when we met large trucks and buses on some of the sharper mountain curves where our outer set of tires dropped off of the pavement. Whichever of us was seated on the outside would gasp each time that happened, because that person could not see any pavement or shoulder of the road, just treetops as the sharply sloped part of the mountain fell away. It definitely was a breathtaking experience.

As usual, when we travelled for LEAD, we were at the mercy of someone else's decision making. On one occasion, as we returned to Visak, I was aware that the driver seemed to be in a hurry. The tires complained around most of the curves. I also noticed that he used his transmission to gear down for some other curves. I suggested that we slow down as we had no deadline to meet in Visak. He gave a tersely polite answer but did not alter his speed. Barbara and I prayed, held on more tightly and occasionally patted each other's hand. When we finally arrived at the bottom of the mountain, the driver parked the car by a small creek. He got a bucket out of the trunk and proceeded to cool off the front wheels. Only then did I understand that he had brake problems but he could not afford to lose this good fare. Fortunately, nothing else was lost that day either. When we arrived at the Green Star Hotel, it was definitely a time of rejoicing for us.

Being There

Being in Araku Valley with Wayne's leaders was a sugarplum experience in every way, with one exception. The guestroom where the LEAD teachers stayed was barebones and had little toward creature comforts. A double bed dominated the space with no closet or drawer spaces available. The bed was challenging, to say the least. It felt as if a drunk person had laid out a wavy, cement driveway then cut a piece of it to be used as a mattress for this bed. We actually placed a pillow against our backs, while lying on our sides, in order to have something soft to lie up against. There were two nails that had been driven into the back of one door on which to hang clothes. Fortunately, there was a small table with two straight-backed chairs in the room which allowed us a place to use our computer when needed. The bathroom, likewise, was utilitarian. It had a water tank for splash baths and a squat pot. The design did not include a sink, but there was a small mirror nailed to the wall beside the water tank. Being at a higher elevation also meant that the bath water in the tank was quite cold. Blessedly, the kitchen heated water, upon request, to add to the bath water. There never was any justified fear of being scalded by this added water, but it did take the edge off and kept our teeth from chattering. All of this added fuel to the growing antici-pation of that Friday night bath waiting for us at the Green Park Hotel.

Our food was delicious. Wayne and Linda sent their cook from Visak to prepare meals for the LEAD team and our translators. We were served in a separate dining room from the attendees. We had a nice table, porcelain plates, and silverware. On the second or third visit to Araku Valley, Barbara and I insisted on eating the noon meal with the LEAD participants. The staff was afraid that as Westerners it would be too difficult for us to sit on the floor, eat from tin plates or off banana leaves, and use only our fingers as utensils. They also said that the partic-ipants would be greatly embarrassed if we joined them. After a struggle, we prevailed and joined our brothers and sisters, which immediately yielded a more intimate fellowship. As we all ate, we laughed, we joked, and we bonded. Yes, we also had to be helped up off the floor sometimes after sitting on the hard concrete for thirty to forty-five minutes.

On one of the early trips to the Araku Valley, against warnings from Wayne and staff, I decided to climb up a portion of the mountain behind Wayne's compound. They had said something about mountain lions and panthers, but I had planned for only a short jaunt. I found an outcropping of a boulder and sat there for a while, communing with God in deep appreciation for such beauty before me. As I rose, I suddenly saw a paw print in the dirt beside the boulder. There were others, as well. What really got my attention was how wide the prints were; much wider than my hand. I began to imagine just how big a cat would need to be to make such a paw print. I also realized the cat had gone out on the same piece of rock on which I had been sitting. I imagined that cat probably being thankful for all of those "two-legged dinners" walking around down below. Needless to say, I scurried back down the mountain, never to return again. And, yes, I was told by the staff that the night watchman had observed a large black panther stroll lazily through the compound a week before. From then on, I appreciated the mountain views from inside a car or van as we travelled back and forth from Visakhapatnam to the Araku Valley.

Wayne and Linda Joseph remained two of our favorite beautiful Giants as they ministered to an entire valley that hosted nine tribal groups, two-hundred-fifty orphaned children and a fine group of evangelist/church planters. Isaiah would have been very proud of the feet of these two Giants.

18

HUMBLE GIANT
ON THE PLANTATION

The measuring tape that Jesus uses to determine greatness is servant-hood. According to our Lord, the more a person serves in His kingdom's work, the greater that person becomes in Jesus' kingdom (Matthew 20:26). Jesus could have been looking down the byways of time thinking of Yohanes Haryono as a prime example of that truth.

Pastor Yohanes (John) is one of the greatest illustrations of servant-leadership I have ever encountered. He seemed heaven-bent on aiding someone during each minute of every day of his life. Yohanes was loved or hated, according from which side of the cross he was viewed. Yohanes' church members loved him because he was constantly doing things to benefit them. The local Muslims hated him because he was also doing good things for his Muslim friends and neighbors, a number of whom had been attracted to Christ because of him.

Yohanes first arrived in Muko-Muko ten years before LEAD started teaching seminars there. The vast majority of people in Muko-Muko were fiery, Sumatran Muslims. They immediately forbade Yohanes to preach or even attend the small Baptist church that he had been called to pastor. They confronted him and his family in the front yard of his house with shouts and threats, hoping to scare him into returning immediately to Java. They were not prepared for this soft-spoken man of God who went out and faced them.

Rather than argue with them, Yohanes squatted down and sat on his heels as he explained that his God had sent him and his family to live there with them to be of any help he could be to them. The locals demanded that he not go into the church building to preach or teach. Yohanes said that he understood and would comply until they changed their minds. The group left and for the next six months, Yohanes did not go into his church building. What he did for the next six months was teach one of his church members what to preach and how to preach each week. He also taught Bible studies from his front porch to his church members who sat in his front yard. His wife, Ibu (Mrs.) Yohanes, (in Indonesia the wife often is called by her husband's first name) each Saturday taught Sunday school teachers how to teach children the Bible before the following Sunday.

Pastor and Mrs. Yohanes also visited every home in their area, both Christian and Muslim. They often organized assistance from their church for various crises that came to families, both Christian and Muslim alike. There were a few times when the survival of one of these families depended on that aid, be it food or sometimes even money. After six months, a committee from the Muslim political group informed Yohanes that he could start preaching in his church. They said, "It didn't do any good to keep you out of the church because you just brought the church out where you were. You might as well go in so the church will maybe stay in the church now." It didn't, because Yohanes continued to lead by example in serving anyone that had a need, be they Christian or Muslim. God blessed this faith community and they ended up having to enlarge the church building.

Four years after the Haryonos arrived in Muko-Muko, Yohanes was invited to serve on Muko-Muko's Community Council. He was the first Christian to have ever been allowed to join that council. Apparently, a number of Muslim families pressured the council to invite Yohanes to join because he, or some of his church members, brought food over to their homes when a wife or mother had gotten malaria, or did some of the farming work when a husband or father was injured. Yohanes humbly accepted the honor and served for years afterwards in that position.

Pastor Yohanes had an open-door policy concerning all he did in ministry either with his church or with the LEAD seminars. He invited every pastor of all denominations in the area to the LEAD seminars. It was one of the most diverse groups we taught anywhere. In fact, Baptist leaders were in the minority. From the beginning, those who attended knew that we were Baptist, but they desperately wanted to understand their Bibles better, so they came. Without it being said, we all decided to major on the truths that bound us together and not emphasize issues that separated us. Pastor Yohanes was the key. He was so loving and caring that it was just plain hard to argue with him. And they didn't.

Pastor Ai, from a large Assembly of God church, gave a testimony at the end of one week. One of the subjects that we studied that week was titled, "How to Prepare a Biblical Sermon." Pastor Ai, a true man of God and well respected in the group, said with tears in his eyes, "I've never prepared the Word of God like this. I promise you, my church members, and Almighty God, that I will never step behind the pulpit unprepared again." In the following seminar six months later, Pastor Ai was on "cloud nine" because his church had become alive and had started growing again. He credited it to the instruction he had received on how to prepare God's Word as the primary reason for the change. Then he turned to Yohanes and gave him a bear hug in appreciation for having been invited to study God's Word in Yohanes' church.

Yohanes was a blur during each week of the LEAD seminars. He would have taken his wife to the market each morning by 5 a.m. He would then help start the cleaning process of the food until some of the church ladies came to help prepare the meals for the day. Every morning the church building was swept and arranged by Pastor Yohanes. He then attended each teaching session for six-and-a-half hours a day. After the final session, he went and bought gasoline for the generator that provided lights for the night activities, which included doing nightly a homework assignment. Sometimes he helped some of the lesser educated pastors and leaders by giving extra explanations, and always assisted them with their homework. There were nights when it was after midnight before he got back home.

Early one morning, about 2 a.m., we were awakened by our bed being jostled. Since Barbara and I had been in a number of earthquakes, we knew exactly what was happening. Before we could get out of bed, it stopped. We turned over and went back to sleep just as a heavy downpour of rain began. When we arose and went to breakfast the next morning, we discovered that Yohanes had jumped up and gone over to the church building, concerned about possible damage. He discovered some of the clay roof tiles had been jarred out of place and broken by the tremors, causing leaks. In the driving rain, with only a flashlight, he repaired the roof. Then he and some of the awakened pastors cleaned up the wet areas. The pastors returned to sleep but Yohanes went over to check on his closest neighbors and helped them put plastic tarps over their roofs until they could buy more roof tiles. After breakfast that morning, I suggested he take the morning off and get some well-deserved sleep. His answer was, "Oh no, Mr. Harry. I need to know more about what we are going to study this morning. Also, my group will give a report and I must be there."

It was such an honor to stand beside this humble Giant on the palm oil plantation in Muko-Muko. We were continually challenged by his example of selfless love for others throughout every day of his life. According to Jesus, this was one of the greatest men I've ever known.

GETTING THERE

The first step toward getting to Muko-Muko is to fly into Bengkulu, located on the southwest tip of Sumatra, Indonesia. We always spent a night, going and coming, in the Horizon Hotel, which was a plus by any standard.

The car lurched out of the hotel's parking lot early Sunday mornings as the trip consumed between seven to nine hours. Road conditions changed like the weather. We took one of the two trans-Sumatran highways; the west coast one. However, being two lanes, it was far below American interstate standards. During the fall rainy season, potholes often became pot-bogs. The hole could expand to the size of a shopping center where you could lose two large trucks. Smaller vehicles tried to go around it over rough and rocky terrain. Some parts of the highway broke off when it came too close to the lapping ocean. Each trip had its unique challenges; some were major ones.

On one occasion we were stopped by a tangle of traffic. The axiom governing Asian traffic must be remembered: "No space is allowed to remain vacant; it must be filled." That meant, when your side of the road was cluttered with stopped cars, you must go to the other side of the road and do likewise. That was the situation of the tangle when we arrived. I never did understand what caused the tangle but after a long time, apparently it became untangled, but to no avail as there were vehicles covering all spaces on both sides of the road. A Texas standoff would be an appropriate description of that perfect logjam. It took more than an hour to work out a pathway going in opposite directions before the lanes became normal again. The entire process was accompanied with amplified voices shouting insults at one another. Finally wormholes were made so the traffic began to trickle forward again. We always sighed in relief when we worked through these obstacles. Movement meant the wind could start drying off our dripping faces again.

In 2007, after a powerful earthquake pancaked numerous buildings all along the coastal highway, the trip took even longer. The scenes were surreal because the roofs were sitting, intact, on the floors of their houses. Seemingly, powerful monsters had kicked out the walls simultaneously and allowed the heavy tiled roofs to crash to the floor, killing all under its load. Another amazing thing we saw on that trip was the end of a bridge over a medium-sized river that had been moved about twelve inches. It appeared as if a huge giant had lifted up one end of the bridge and dropped it back down again twelve inches to one side. Not far from that bridge, a section of the paved highway had been eaten by the earth underneath it. It was in an area close to the ocean where the highway was no more. We used the temporary trail beside that crushed-in area where the road had been. The awesome power that could move bridges, pancake houses and government buildings, and toss multistoried mosques about like empty milk bottles was beyond defining.

We were always overjoyed when we arrived at Pastor Yohanes' home in Muko-Muko. We were ready to get out of the car, ready to get a cold splash-bath, and ready to get settled into our room for the week so that we could get focused on what we were about to start teaching the following morning. Pastor Yohanes always received us so graciously and made us feel like we had just arrived home again, and in some ways, we had.

BEING THERE

Pastor Yohanes' house was perched on the side of the main clay road of the Muko-Muko Palm Oil Plantation. This road ran from the entrance of the plantation to—and through—a set of government offices overseeing the production of palm oil in Muko-Muko. The road was always dusty, or muddy, depending on whether it was rainy season or not. All houses and few shops along the road were built close to the road while being surrounded on the other three sides with palm trees. These trees were set out in groves with walking lanes in between each row. The affect was a canopy of shade extending as far as you could see.

We stayed in the pastor's house in Kesia's room, their preteen daughter. The house was constructed out of roughhewn wood with a cement floor. The interior walls were also made from the same materials. This was a very rural setting in all aspects. Our room was about eleven-by-eleven feet. There was about two-and-a-half feet of floor space at the foot of the bed and three feet down one side of the bed. The rest of the room was filled with a bed. It was comfortable enough but had no top sheet. There was a clothes-tree on which to hang a few things, plus two nails in the wall. Two small windows were placed in the center of the outer wall, with no screens, but a curtain for privacy. Of course, there was nothing to see out the windows but rows of palm trees marching up a small hill separating the pastor's house from the church. We placed our personal items on the two-by-four horizontal wall studs along the walls, as there was no tabletop space available. Electricity was not available in the daytime, but a small generator ran at night from about six until ten o'clock to provide lights and such. The bathroom consisted of a raised up, cement squat-pot toilet, and a *bak*, a cement water tank for splash baths using a handheld dipper. The bathroom was dark at night and crowded in the morning, as all six of us needed to use it at about the same time. Each night, when the generator stopped, Pastor Yohanes placed small oil lamps in both the bathroom and on the dining room table to light the way to the bathroom. Their family closed all windows and doors but we kept our windows open day and night. There were some mosquitoes but we used mosquito coils and it seemed to keep the bombers off of us. Often we sat in the sitting room at night to study or read. We opened the doors and windows there at night, which meant we needed to use a mosquito coil there as well.

Pak Yohanes' servanthood genes had transferred down to his children, Agus, his fifteen-year-old son and Kesia, his daughter. Upon returning home from school, both would change clothes and go to work. Kesia would go to the house next to the church building where the food was being prepared for the seminar participants. She would just blend in with whatever needed to be done and work until after the evening meal was served and all was cleaned up afterwards. Kesia's mom, Ibu Yohanes, was in charge of all of the food procurement and preparation. She was one of the hardest working persons I've ever seen. Agus, on the other hand, grabbed a machete or some other tools and went out into Pastor Yohanes' personal palm tree grove. The pastor had to farm palm trees for oil in order to live, as the church could not provide for all of his needs. Therefore during the week of the seminar, Agus did most of the farming from after school until well after dark. Kesia would bring home a plate of food for his supper from the eating house. Then, while the generator was functioning, both of these sharp young people did their homework on the kitchen table underneath a single fifty-watt bulb which was dropped down from the ceiling. We considered the Haryono family one of the premiere families we have ever met anywhere on earth. They excelled in every category except wealth. However, they were rich beyond means when using God's measurements for true wealth.

Each time we were privileged to serve in Muko-Muko our hearts soared heavenward. We counted it a pure delight to walk beside such a giant as Pastor Yohanes as he not only preached the gospel, but lived it out loud minute by minute, day in and day out.

19

THE BROWN ANGEL WITH GRIT

"Mista Harry, you jest have ta come to Bandarugudem and teach my workers. You jest have ta!" said what appeared to be a brown angel. Pastor Jacob could have been in Bollywood (India's Hollywood) with his handsome face, raven-black hair, fiery eyes, and flashing, Pepsodent smile. I had already said "sorry" to Jacob four other times because of the lack of teachers to meet the growing demand to equip rural and inner-city pastors in India. Jacob had travelled six arduous hours in order to persuade "Mr. and Mrs. Harry" to take LEAD's ministry to Bandarugudem located in the heart of the Indian subcontinent.

When Jacob was a preteen, he contracted an undiagnosed disease. His family lived in South India on good farmland. Jacob was taken to a rural hospital and soon told that the doctors could not do anything for his condition. At that point his parents were told, "Take him home and keep him comfortable until…." That very night, Jacob had an experience. He was not sure if it was real, a dream, or a vision. He saw a Man, in gleaming white apparel, coming to him, calling his name. The Man identified Himself as Jesus and said that He was going to heal Jacob. Then Jesus said, "Afterwards, follow Me." To the utter amazement of the doctors, Jacob was healed and sent home the next day.

Jacob's mother and father were nominal Christians, so they sought out a nearby church to ask what all of this meant. The pastor of that small rural church led Jacob to Christ and Jacob, his parents, and older siblings were baptized in that church. Jacob started following Jesus and growing in his young faith. God called him to spread the gospel, so Jacob went to a Bible school. While there, God called him to go to the tribal areas where the gospel was basically unknown. Jacob's call was heard down through each member of his family. His father sold his producing farm and searched out land up in the region of Bandarugudem where a number of the Koya tribe lived. The whole family moved. Jacob had married by this time and had one child. Jacob's mother and father bought land close to the Koya people and started farming to help support Jacob as he began to target this tribal group.

God breathed on Jacob's labors. He started by loving and educating orphans, mixed with a clear-eyed, bold-voiced proclamation of God's Word. These efforts resulted in a church, and then another, only to be followed by many others. In ten years after 1991, the ministry to which Jacob gave birth, The Gospel for the Tribals, baptized 10,016 souls while starting and developing one-hundred-eighty churches. Jacob desperately needed help in training his growing leadership.

When we arrived at Jacob's compound, "unimpressive" didn't do justice to our first impression. But the second impression was much more powerful. A score of kids of all sizes scampered up to our car with smiles ablaze as they sang and shouted a joyous welcome. They were quickly followed by Pastor Jacob—who constantly wore one of the little ones around his neck—and a large group of his workers. All came with warm greetings and helpful hands. Her Highness, the Queen of England, could not have received a more royal greeting. It made the price of the ticket well worth it.

The kids were orphans, or with one parent who could not afford to raise them. They ranged in age from babies to about sixteen-years-old.

We'd get to play with them before breakfast and after supper, but during the day, we taught biblical truths to thirty of Jacob's handpicked workers. These participants were pastors, church planters, and orphanage workers. They were a delight to teach and were like proverbial sponges, soaking up all we could give them.

Early one morning about midweek on our third teaching visit, we found Pastor Jacob sitting by the outside cooking fire. It was the first time I'd ever seen him without his smile. He was somber; clearly disturbed. We inquired about an obvious problem. He pulled a ragged piece of paper from his Bible and read it to us with a quivering voice, as the note was in a local dialect: "Get rid of the foreigners. Send all of the children away or we'll come and burn all of you in one of your buildings. Signed: The RSS." The RSS were noted gangs of young fanatical Hindu thugs and killers who terrorized rural Indians, especially Christians and Muslims. We didn't have to ask if the note was valid, for his saddened eyes and firm jaw confirmed it.

"What do you want to do?" I inquired. "Do you want us to leave right now?" Jacob said he would ask God for an answer and tell us at lunchtime. It was a long four hours of teaching and waiting.

At lunch, we gathered with Jacob and Elizabeth, his wife. He looked to be at peace. He simply said, "The Got (God) told me before to make a place for hurting children. The Got gave me the children and then the workers. The Got has not told me to stop. So we stay! Where can my little ones go? Where can my brothers and sisters go? We stay! The Got will protect us." Then he added, "But if you need to go, we all understand."

I said, "The Got didn't tell us to go either; we are staying, too." He embraced me and pumped Barbara's hand up and down vigorously, and said, "Let's eat; we have classes this afternoon." We left on Friday as planned. No harm ever came to Jacob or his little ones. As we pulled out I told Barbara, "There's a brown angel with grit."

Getting There

Bandarugudem is not highlighted on any maps for tourist destinations in India. We flew into Hyderabad, the capital city of the state of Andhra Pradesh in Central India. Then it required six hours of sweltering heat in an open-windowed car. Road paste was applied to our faces, necks, and arms, hour by hour. The paste consisted of our rolling sweat mixed with swirls of oily dirt that plastered us through each open window. That application process took upwards of seven hours, dictated by the traffic snarls in some of the towns, plus the number of goat and cattle herds we had to crawl through as they lumbered down the middle of the two-lane highways.

For the first four seminars, Jacob had sent one of his workers to guide the drivers to Bandarugudem, as none of them had ever heard of that metropolis. Bathroom breaks came at a premium and were prearranged by Jacob. Most were in small eating places. Some actually had doors and windows, but not most. However, all of them had an enclosed toilet facility with the standard squatty-potty. There was water available in each bathroom to clean yourself and especially your left hand. These establishments also offered hot tea or coffee with a few rice and dishes of dahl, a spicy stew-like dish made from lentils. Rarely would there be anything cold to drink because ice was not readily available. We were constantly warned about using ice because it was made from unhygienic water, like the water in the ditches beside the road. The temptation to order an iced drink was unbelievably powerful. The only way we overcame that temptation was from the vivid memories of trying to travel in India with a case of diarrhea. Not a pretty picture, and something we would avoid at all cost.

The rolling side view from our car was color coded. There were two primary colors: green and dirty brown. The presence of water made a stark difference. Water was the "kingmaker." Water issued forth life, and in abundance in some cases. Wherever a stream of water meandered through, there came a "green tail" wagging behind it. Water from wells was hand carried to plants in the furrows which infused them with life. But in the arid, waterless areas, the ground lay parched. In those places, sometimes vast open lands, there was no life; no villages; no animals. That land seemed to ache for life. It was a mural of the spiritual lostness in India.

As water was the kingmaker, each king, therefore, made their own kingdom in a way that reflected the cornerstone of the Indian social structure. That cornerstone was the "outlawed" caste system. Outlawed or not, the caste system was obvious in every stitch of the social fabric of India. Even out in the hinterlands of India, alongside the tiny byways, you saw large, substantial houses followed down the pecking order to shacks made of mud and straw. The sons and daughters, born and raised in those houses or shacks, never changed in status but remained the same, generation by generation; locked in by the invisible, predetermined chain of their caste.

As we neared Bandarugudem, the area greened-up significantly. The small town became apparent, with Jacob's compound on the southern outskirts. What a beautiful sight it was. We had finally arrived and could now get out of the sandblaster.

BEING THERE

Being in Bandarugudem was an absolute joy, but rife with plenty of challenges. Heat was one of those challenges. It was hot every time we went to Bandarugudem, which was in the spring and then the fall. In the springtime, it was dry and sizzling hot, day and night. However, in the fall, the rainy season was coming to an end, though there would still be an occasional shower. Those would produce sweaty nights as the air felt muggy and heavy. Heat sucked out our energy like a celestial vacuum cleaner. There would be many a night that we'd have to get up and apply wet washcloths to our soaked bodies, just to cool them down.

We were always given the best of everything that they had in Bandarugudem. In fact, we stayed in Jacob and Elizabeth's own bedroom. They moved out for that week to let us have their place. It was the only private place on the compound. The room had two sections in it; the front had a door and small window. It was a small sitting room with a little coffee table surrounded by four wooden chairs. The table was covered by a cloth tablecloth with pretty flowers embroidered on it. There were always freshly picked flowers sitting in the middle in a clear drinking glass. The two sections of the room were separated by a wooden wall. A piece of cloth functioned as a door leading into a medium-sized bedroom. The lack of any windows in that room got your attention immediately. No windows meant little light and no moving air. That registered loud and clear in our minds. The nine-foot ceiling helped, but a full day of scorching sunshine outside produced heat on the inside. That heat just stacked downward until it nestled nicely upon the bed, making an invisible blanket ready to wrap you up as soon as you fell onto the bed. The mattress was one that you slept on and not in. But that was just fine considering the heat factor.

Fortunately, Jacob had a small, oscillating fan available for us. It was an absolute lifesaver. We placed it on one of the wooden chairs and it moved the hot air over us but with a degree of coolness unachieved by anything else. However, since the electricity was unreliable, especially at night, we'd often start with some moving air only to wake up drenched in sweat.

Another reason Jacob and Elizabeth gave us their room was that they had the only private bathroom on the compound. All others were for the males and females who lived and worked there. Our (Jacob's) bathroom was connected to the bedroom section. The bathroom was a small room with a squatty-potty and a bak, a cement water container used for both toilet needs and taking baths. This container was about three-feet long, two-feet wide and about four-feet deep. Since there was no running water, it was filled daily, as were all of the baks. Each bak had a dipper provided and that is how you took your baths. You dipped that cooled (sometimes chilled) water out of the bak and poured it over you. There is not a more delicious feeling in the world than pouring cool water over yourself when you have been soaked in sweat for most of the day and night. It was so refreshing, so cleansing; an absolute delight.

The electricity was out so much that we always had small oil lamps lit in the bathroom and in our bedroom. Of course, there were plenty of mosquitoes, but our burning mosquito coils usually kept them buzzing about five feet up from the floor. We used a lot of batteries each week we were in Bandarugudem as you needed to see where you were putting your feet when you got up to go to the bathroom at night. There were crawly things, hoppy things, and a few slithering things that you did not want to step on. Each night was an adventure of its own.

The blessings always outweighed the challenges. Each morning and evening we'd get a chance to play with the children, tell them stories (translated, of course) and just love on them. There was no greater reward than to hold a precious little hand of one who had already known more pain that most human beings accumulate in a lifetime and just be a safe place for her. We were safe because we were an extension of Papa Jacob or Mama Elizabeth. What joy it was to let them sit in your lap and rub on your white skin and see them shudder with glee. We encouraged the older ones and gave them vision of being and accomplishing far beyond anything they had experienced in that restricted area. What a privilege it was!

Our blessings were compounded and multiplied each time we were privileged to be with Jacob's pastors/church planters and workers. Jacob had chosen thirty men and women from his group to be trained by LEAD. We observed their faithful commitment to the Bible as God's own Word to all of us. They also exhibited wonderful exuberance in each moment of worship and service that we shared. Truly each of these thirty leaders were Giants in and of themselves, led by two other extraordinary Giants of the faith, Jacob and Elizabeth.

20

THE OVERCOMING GIANTS

This chapter will take a different form from all the others. There will be no "Getting There" or "Being There" sections. Barbara and I were not directly involved in this account. However, we were involved with the family who experienced the following terrifying experiences because Ella, the mother in this chapter, is our "heart-adopted daughter" from Indonesia. The following true account is about what happened to Ella and Joiy Lempas, and their fourteen-month-old daughter, Fena, in November 1999.

SITUATION ON THE ISLAND OF TERNATE, EASTERN INDONESIA, IN NOVEMBER 1999:

Sporadic news reports of bloody clashes between radical Islamists and Christians on some islands in East Indonesia began increasing in late 1999. Rumors barked everywhere of shiploads of Islamic warriors running wild on the island of Ambon, which was not very far from the island of Ternate where Joiy and Ella lived. Articles stated that blood flowed in the gutters of Ambon like rainwater after a storm. The word on the street was that Ternate was the next target of the Islamists.

Joiy and Ella, home missionaries of their Baptist convention, were planting a church six kilometers (almost four miles) out in a rural section across a mountain from the capital city of Ternate. Ternate was the name of the capital city as well as the island itself. The Lempas family did not own a personal vehicle, not even a motorcycle, therefore they were totally dependent on public transportation. Their hearts began doing backflips with anxiety at that time. Should they take their precious baby, Fena (named Trifena from Romans 16:12), and flee, or stay as a witness for their Almighty God? The little Lempas family felt like they were in an emotional earthquake where nothing was stable or safe anymore. On a visit with a fellow pastor friend in the city of Ternate, his adamant advice was, "Go home, pack a few clothes, grab some rice, and come back here to our house to stay for a while. We can get to the harbor very quickly from here and escape, if needed." The commercial harbor was the safest spot on Ternate as it had a contingent of police there and boats could always be hired to go to other nearby islands. Joiy and Ella finally agreed. They went home planning to pack a few things, let some church members know of their plans and return to the city that evening. Joiy also wanted to tell his neighbors about the latest possible imminent attack because many Christians lived in their very large neighborhood. Their plans did not work out as hoped.

NOVEMBER 5, 1999; 4 P.M.:

After arriving at their house in the afternoon, Ella gathered up what they would need as Joiy shared the word with his neighbors. This was the largest concentration of Christians on Ternate, so it took a while. One older husband and wife who attended their church and lived a couple of dirt streets over from them wanted to come and spend the night with the Lempases. They were visibly frightened. Joiy and Ella agreed, as it was already late afternoon and would be dark before they could return to the city. After all, what was one more night? The shadows were closing in on them and it was getting ever darker.

The older couple arrived carrying a small bag of clothes and a partial sack of uncooked rice. The Lempases had the same things, except Joiy put their belongings in his small backpack. No one had an appetite but Ella tried to feed Fena. The baby had become increasingly agitated, no doubt sensing Ella's anxiety. They didn't turn on any lights that night. No one wanted to change into bedclothes as it became obvious that there would be little to no sleep for anyone in the Lempas household. Joiy suggested that they spend some time in prayer, which had a calming effect. All continued to pray silently after the verbal prayer time had ended. Ella finally got Fena down in her crib. She remembered looking at Fena's beautifully formed, round face with her dark eyelashes snuggled tightly shut. She prayed, "Oh, my dear Lord and God, don't let anything harm my precious baby. Keep her safe in Your mighty arms." No one, except Fena, slept that night.

They remembered an eerie silence that hushed down upon the Lempas household and throughout their neighborhood as though a thick quilt was let down from the sky and muffled every outside sound. The silence advertised that there were no vehicles moving, no night birds calling out, no screeching owls; not even one dog barking. It seemed as if even the mice in the ceiling had pads on their feet. Ella felt like the world had tilted upward and everything, including them, had slid down into a silenced, cushioned corner. Fear glistened on each of their faces as they waited, moment by moment, for a hint of sunrise in the eastern sky.

NOVEMBER 6, 1999; 3 A.M.:

Ring-ring! The phone shattered the silence in the Lempas household before dawn and Joiy snatched up the receiver. "Get out! Get out of your house now!" shouted the urgent voice of their pastor friend in the city. He urged them to get into the city immediately. He reported that some of his church members who owned fishing vessels in the commercial harbor had just called and told him that all of their boats were ablaze at that very moment. Joiy spoke to him for a moment more and then all of the adults went out into the Lempas' front yard. They were met with that scary quietness. The hairs on the back of their necks stood at attention. Again, there were no audible sounds. The black silence took on an aura of evil, threatening anything that moved or spoke. It was clear that no public vehicles were running and that they could not walk four miles over the peak of the mountain in pitch darkness, so they returned to the living room. With tears and muffled sobs, they pleaded with their God for His protection.

NOVEMBER 6, 1999; 5:30 A.M.:

Voices started shouting from the street just before sunrise, "All Christians go to the Halmahera Church." The Kepala Kampung (government-appointed neighborhood leader) and his associates, who were all Muslims, instructed the Christians to gather at the newly constructed church building which was about two blocks away. These leaders told the fleeing Christians that some Muslim radicals had come to the island during the previous night, but that they, the local Muslim leaders, would protect their Christian neighbors. They had ordered a military truck to come from the harbor to rescue them. The truck was on the way and would be there shortly.

As Joiy, Ella, Fena, and their neighbors started out of their house, they discovered that the handle of their front door had been broken. The door would not open until Joiy yanked hard on the handle. It came apart in his hand and the door finally opened. Someone had tried to sneak into their house after 3 a.m. when they had earlier gone out into the front yard. Only after they had gotten to the church and mingled with the others did Joiy and Ella understand the full significance of the broken handle. The Jihadist group had put the word out that they would pay fifty million Rupiah ($4,000) for each severed head of a Christian pastor. It would be like someone who makes $10 an hour getting paid $270,000 for a cut-off head of a pastor. Very tempting. Very terrifying. As Joiy and Ella absorbed what almost happened during the previous evening, they immediately praised God for His evident hand of protection.

About fifty Christian neighbors gathered to wait at the pastor's house of the Halmahera Church rather than in the church building itself. The pastor did not want to mess up the newly constructed church building as it had just been completed and was about to be dedicated during the worship service on the following Sunday morning.

NOVEMBER 6, 1999; 9 A.M.:

"Allahu akbar!… allahu akbar!" (God is great!) The war cry came wafting into the pastor's house that was crammed with fifty people. They had been instructed to get inside and stay until the truck arrived. Joiy and Ella, holding Fena, stampeded out into the front yard. Their blood froze. They saw a group of young men pouring gasoline over the new church building. All of these men were sporting the white bandanas indicating that they were the front prong of the invading Islamic warriors. These young men were dancing and whooping, "Allahu akbar!" Then the group of Christians saw the road leading down to a second harbor, which was an inlet where a lot of their Christian neighbors had fishing vessels. It was a curvy road. At that present moment the road was filled with what seemingly was an army of white-banded warriors surging upward from the water toward their neighborhood. It appeared to be an evil, white-speckled snake slithering toward them. Each one of the warriors had a weapon—spears, machetes, long-knives and a few hand guns. All were chillingly chanting, "Kill the Christians…kill the dogs."

Joiy instantly shouted, "Betrayed! We've been betrayed!" Others had come to the same conclusion. The supposed benevolent Muslim leaders of their neighborhood had intentionally deceived the Christians into thinking they were going to be rescued when, in fact, the plan was to slaughter them or burn them alive together in the new church building. A group of men from the group of Christians grabbed up pieces of fencing, rocks and poles as they ran forward to confront this first surge of the invading mass, hoping to give a little time for their wives and kids to escape being hacked to death.

Joiy shouted, "Ayo!" ("Come on!") as he led about forty women, children, and a few older folks down an embankment. They all had to negotiate a four-foot fence to get away. Joiy led the small, fleeing group of Christians to another Christian's house that fronted on the only road of escape which went up over the peak of the mountain. After clearing the peak that road meandered through a number of switchback curves and dropped into the entrance of the commercial harbor. There was safety at the harbor because of the large contingent of policemen that were assigned to protect the harbor. That road was their only hope. They needed to get to where the police could protect them and where they could get a boat off of the island of Ternate. But time was running out.

Little eyes, full of terror and tears, peered around their mama's sarongs and skirts as they hid in the house. There were muffled screams of abject fear escaping many lips sounding like a discordant pipe organ. Also spewing into this chaos were angry shouts of betrayal, while others tried to give encouragement to bolster the courage of these men and women fleeing for their lives. The small house was not made to contain forty pushing, hysterical people. They spilled out into the bamboo fenced backyard with nowhere else to go. Joiy was desperate. They had to get over that peak, but how? He looked at Ella, who was crying and Fena screaming in unknowable terror. She sensed her world was ripping apart but was too young to comprehend why.

NOVEMBER 6, 1999; 9:30 A.M.:

"Look, smoke!" someone shouted. Again, the crowd pushed back out into the front yard. The entire sky, in the direction of the church building, and where many Christian homes were, began to darken with billowing black puffs boiling upward. It looked like the entire edge of the world had sparked into raging flames. Joiy frantically looked at his wife and baby daughter. Fena was squalling. Tears streaked Ella's face but her lips were in constant motion. Joiy knew she was pleading with their heavenly Father. He glanced again up the only route of escape and if as by magic; no, not magic, but more likely by a heavenly response, there appeared a slowly moving vehicle. Joiy shouted over the cacophony of terrified screams to Ella, "Get the women and children to that tree beside the road over there." He turned and started sprinting uphill toward the pickup truck which was slowly easing its way down the curvy road.

As the truck entered the straight part of the road that dropped into their neighborhood, Joiy saw it was a police pickup with two sets of bench seats in its bed. He leaped in front of it forcing the truck to stop. They informed him that they were on a peacekeeping mission and could not help carry the women and children back to the harbor. Joiy screamed at them, "Look! See those fires of ten to twenty houses and churches burning? There are at least a thousand of them and just the two of you. There's not going to be any peacemaking; only slaughter if you don't get our wives and children out of here!" The police drove down to the tree, turned around and loaded up the women and children. They shoehorned twenty of them into the back of that pickup.

"We're not leaving you, Jo," cried Ella. She was refusing to get in the back of the truck in the slot that Joiy had saved for her.

"Manisku" ("My Sweetie"), you must! Do you want me to see my wife and baby hacked to death in front of me? Get in. Then I can think about my escape but don't stop praying," pleaded Joiy with eyes brimming over with tears. Ella climbed into the back of the truck. Some men helped push the truck off as the heavy weight in the back made it difficult to get started uphill. Joiy stared at that precious spot in the back of the police pickup until it vanished out of sight as it went around the first curve.

Ella prayed for her Jo. Fena was quickly soothed into quietness by the rocking of the truck. There were sobs and groans emitted by those who were on their way to safety but had left, like Ella, a husband or loved one in harm's way. Suddenly they rounded the last curve before the peak and there was a mob of local Muslim men. They were waving weapons in the air. Apparently they were waiting for the mass of invaders to get up to them. These men immediately saw the uncovered heads of the women and knew they were Christians trying to escape the purge.

They shouted aggressively, "Bunuh lonte!" ("Kill the whores"). The mob became crazed, screaming while jumping up and down. They stumbled toward the slowly moving truck which suddenly stalled. Ella screamed and leaned over Fena trying to protect her from being hacked to pieces. She quickly uttered a prayer for God's help. Looking backwards toward the crowd, Ella was amazed to see the Muslim wives running out and grabbing ahold of their husbands. They loudly pleaded, "Don't hurt these women; don't kill the babies." The engine fired up again but the load was too heavy to start moving forward. Ella was utterly shocked when a group of older Muslim men came over and started pushing the truck to get it rolling again. The truck gained power and escaped over the top of the mountain. Ella shuddered with terror but also was enveloped in a glow of joy as she, again, realized that she had just seen the invisible hand of God work through her Muslim neighbors. She drew Fena to her breast and clutched her like life itself.

As the truck moved cautiously downward toward the harbor, Ella was sickened by the numerous bodies lying on the side of the road in large puddles of blood. Most of the corpses had their heads severed from the bodies. Some of the heads were far from the piles of bodies as though they had been kicked like soccer balls. The lifeless heads just stared blankly with ribbons of congealed blood wrapped around the necks. All Ella could think about was if someone was going to find her Jo in that exact condition. Then it dawned on her that this particular butchering of Christians had been done by local Muslims, because the invading mass of Jihadists had not reached that point yet. Her terror doubled because that meant Joiy not only had to evade the Islamic warriors but also local groups of Muslim men who were out to kill Christians. Her guttural response to her escalating fear was, "Oh Dear God, don't let this happen to my Jo; please God, please." She kept on repeating that simple prayer as they descended the mountain.

NOVEMBER 6, 1999; 10 A.M. (ELLA):

The pickup arrived at the harbor behind the perimeter of safety. Ella, Fena, and all the other moms and babies were taken to a large building. It was a military mess hall that had the tables and chairs removed. There were some benches on each side of the building. Inside, Christians were crammed into every nook of the large tin building. Many people were bloodied from their wounds. A number of those wounded had blood puddled underneath the wooden benches on which they reclined. A number of folks wandered around the expansive room screaming hysterically at no one in particular. Other women frantically called out names of husbands and children as they staggered from one clump of people to the next. Others like Ella, sat in corners shaking uncontrollably. Tears cascaded off of Ella's face dampening Fena's clothing. Ella continued to lay her urgent petitions at His throne.

NOVEMBER 6, 1999; 10 A.M. (JOIY):

Joiy saw Ella's pickup make the bend in the road as it disappeared out of sight. He cautiously worked his way through the upper part of the neighborhood; aspiring to get up and over the peak of the mountain. The Islamic horde had dispersed into the huge neighborhood. Joiy heard them chanting, "Allahu akbar." He also heard screams of his fellow Christians who were being discovered and murdered. Joiy crossed another road and literally stumbled across the head of his neighbor, Pak (Mr.) Efendi. His neck had been sawn in two by a machete. One eye bulged out while the other was a bloody socket. A spear had obviously been thrust through it. Joiy had talked to Pak Efendi earlier that morning at the pastor's house. As he ran forward, Joiy came across other bodies of some of the men who had bravely gone out from the church that morning to face the invaders. Joiy instantly realized that he was still breathing, and that some of their wives and babies were enroute to safety because of those bodies strewn around like yesterday's garbage.

Joiy was dodging his way from tree to tree and house to house when his respected Muslim neighbor silently motioned for him to come into his house. The house was built into a slight slope of the mountain. The lower section was protected on three sides by the slope. When Muslim men make their pilgrimage to Mecca, they are honored with the right to wear a white skullcap and are called "Hajis." This neighbor was known in the neighborhood as "Pak Haji." He also had the reputation of being a really goodhearted man. He had married a woman from Christianized Manado, and her Christian brother was a frequent visitor to the neighborhood. Joiy was conflicted. Was this another trap by a Muslim in order to kill him? Or was it a genuine offer of safety in a terribly volatile situation? About that time Pak Haji's brother-in-law came out the front door wearing a white head band and urgently motioned Joiy to come to their house. Joiy felt a calming in his spirit. He took a chance and ran to Pak Haji's house. They ushered him downstairs where there was a kitchen and a bathroom. Pak Haji opened the bathroom door and, to Joiy's great surprise, there were twenty of his Christian neighbors sardined into a space of six-by-nine feet. Pak Haji spoke with a glint in his eye, "They will have to kill me before they can kill you." A small electric fan had been placed in the bathroom to alleviate some of the swelter from the equatorial heat that oppressed them. Joiy and twenty others would have to endure those conditions for at least seven more hours before they could try to escape under the cover of darkness.

God's powerful right arm of protection had not yet been exhausted on that day. Included in that suffocating space of the bathroom were one older couple, two mothers with babies in their arms, three other mothers with four small children and one family which included an eleven-year-old boy who had Downs Syndrome, and a few young men. Throughout that day babies would cry, children would fuss and fight, and the child with Downs Syndrome rocked forward and backward loudly moaning his frustration of being cooped inside that sauna box.

NOVEMBER 6, 1999; 1 P.M. (ELLA):

A Christian policeman, who was one of Joiy's and Ella's close neighbors, found Ella in a corner weeping and praying. She was trying to keep Fena calm. He told her that he was about to go out on patrol to gather up as many bodies as they could in order to have a mass burial. The government was concerned about even worse mutilations and disease. Ella urged her neighbor to look for Joiy. He was wearing a blue, pullover shirt with a white stripe across the chest. When he left, Ella doubled down in her prayers for Joiy's safe return. She mumbled aloud, "Jo, don't leave us alone. I don't know how I can raise Fena by myself. Come back to us!" Fena looked up and peered around the room like she was looking for her daddy to come and pick her up. Ella had no idea just how potent her prayers were. At 4 p.m., the policeman returned with the good news that he had not found Joiy's body anywhere among the piles and piles of corpses that they had retrieved.

NOVEMBER 6, 1999; 1 P.M. (JOIY):

In the early afternoon each one of the group in the small bathroom was dripping sweat on the floor. One of the small children spoke for all when she said, "Pew, Mama, what's that bad smell?" There was a full assault on everyone's nose. Then to their horror, they heard loud voices coming down the steps into the kitchen area. Joiy peeked through the cracked door and saw three Islamic warriors with white bandanas around their heads. They were thirsty after all of their brutal work and were gulping water from Pak Haji's kitchen sink. Joiy saw the fan's electric cord and wondered if they might get suspicious seeing an electrical cord going to the bathroom.

Everyone held their breath, not wanting to draw attention to the bathroom. The three turned and went back up the stairs to continue their onslaught. Throughout the long, sizzling afternoon, that scene was frequently repeated. The warriors had worked up a thirst. Pak Haji's house was an obviously good choice. At any of these precarious times, had a baby cried, child fussed, or the eleven-year-old moaned, all of them would have been instantly butchered. But that did not happen! God's Spirit placed His finger on the eyelids of the babies and soothed them to sleep. He put His finger to the mouths of the children and they quietly sat down and He placed His powerful hand on the young boy, calming him so that he sat down and put his head on his knees. This happened each time! These activities became so startlingly miraculous in the rearview mirror of their memories. During these times, that afternoon, all were so concerned with survival that no one fully noticed; they were just trying to stay alive. But later, each one could only look up and praise Him for His miraculous protection.

Pak Haji announced to this group late in the afternoon that his brother-in-law had been able to contact the police and had a military truck coming to rescue them about 6 p.m. as the sun would then be slipping from the sky. Visible relief and excitement flashed across each face and yet they still had another hour to endure. Just before six, one of the younger men in the bathroom ripped up his white shirt into strips so that each one in the bathroom could put a white band around their head, looking like Pak Haji's brother-in-law and the others swarming around the neighborhood. Tears flowed as each person exited the bathroom and hugged Pak Haji for saving their lives. The group boarded the truck with Joiy being the last one to get in. Safety was just across the peak of the mountain.

There were others in the truck when Joiy's group boarded it. One older man was severely wounded. Joiy recognized him from the area but did not know his name. He moved over and put the man's head in his lap. Joiy talked quietly to him, "Hold on, Sir, we are getting closer." Joiy saw that the man's stomach had been ripped open and his innards were spilling out. He also had several deep gashes on his back, arms, and legs. Blood continued oozing out of each wound and the man's breathing was ragged.

On the downward slope, going through the switchback turns, Joiy saw stacks of bodies. Many were headless. Some of the bodies had been mutilated, not only the removing of heads, arms, and legs but genitals also. Joiy screamed in his heart, "How can human beings do such things? Even animals do not do stuff like that."

NOVEMBER 6, 1999; 7 P.M.:

Joiy's truck arrived inside the safety perimeter at the harbor around 7 p.m. that evening. He quickly got some medical attention for the man he was assisting. He then darted from group to group looking for Ella and Fena. It was like a scene out of a movie: Ella was grieving in the corner when she heard her and Fena's name being yelled out. She looked up and saw Joiy across the room. Ella, clutching Fena close to her heart, ran into Joiy's arms as they met in the middle of the room entangling with many others. For a matter of minutes all they could do was hug and kiss each other while praising God at the same time. Ella became seriously alarmed at seeing the blood all over Joiy's shirt, but he assured her that it was not his blood. They had been separated seven torturous hours, which seemed to them like seven days or even seven weeks. They were all three together again, but it wasn't over yet.

NOVEMBER 9, 1999; THREE DAYS LATER:

Joiy, Ella and hundreds of others had been waiting three days for a rescue ship to arrive from Manado. Each day they observed the increased threats from the massive group of invaders and local Muslims who had gathered just outside the perimeter at the harbor. The Islamic warriors kept shouting their threats over the line of police. "Kill the pigs! Erase all Christian blood from Ternate," came their screams. It was clear to Joiy and Ella that this poised evil snake had the numbers to carry out their threats. Plus, the harbor was full of speedboats manned by those wearing the white bandanas. No one could escape by a small fishing boat.

After three days of mounting tension, a large rescue ship arrived in the harbor. They had brought with them a contingent of Indonesian army personnel armed with rifles to protect the ship. However, it was a long distance from the military mess hall, where the Christians were located, to the dock where the ship was. The outside warriors stepped up their shouts and screams as the ship docked. The Islamic horde became clearly more animated with the arrival of the ship. At that moment, a cavalry troop rode in with drawn swords. They were a part of the Sultan of Ternate's personal bodyguards. The Sultan's position was an honorary one, similar to that of royalty of England. It was not government appointed; in fact, it was an Islamic position, but the Sultan had sent his troops to the harbor to ensure that the Christians got safely on that rescue ship. These mounted guards formed a safe pathway between the building to the dock. Many of the guards waved a warm send-off to their fellow Indonesians, even though they were Christians.

As the Christians boarded the ship, the speedboats started darting in close to the ship and threatened to blow it up. The Captain warned them over his loudspeaker that if any boat came within thirty meters again the occupants would be killed. One boat immediately tested his resolve. Joiy and Ella heard the Captain shout, "Fire!" A volley of shots rang out and all but the driver slumped over dead. There were no more challenges and the ship immediately left to take the Christians back to safety in Manado. Hundreds of Christians escaped with their lives on that day, but every family had lost a family member, loved one, or some neighbors. They also had lost everything that they had owned with the exception of what little they could stuff into a small bag. Without exception, all praised God and thanked their loving heavenly Father on that day. All any of them wanted to do, at that point, was nestle down safely in God's almighty arms and rest.

GIANT-HOOD REVEALED:

This true account of the small Lempas family, up to this point, indicates courage, ingenuity, and a clear dependence on God while being fully human throughout it all. But it does not, necessarily, reveal Giant-hood, as we've sought to describe throughout this book. It was what happened after a mere three months of recuperation in the Christian section of the island of Sulawesi, specifically in Christianized

Manado, that truly signified their status as Giants of the faith. After these three months, Joiy and Ella accepted a church planter's position, offered by their Baptist denomination, in the Islamic-majority city of Balikpapan, in Kalimantan (Borneo). The Lempas' decision to rent a house in the Muslim section of the town was surprising to even their own leadership. They simply stated, "People don't often change because they hear the truth, but rather when they see it—the gospel lived out— then it has a larger impact." Truer nor braver words have not been spoken.

Barbara and I held LEAD seminars for the fruit of their ministry (and many others) in this city. We taught men and women who had been captured by Jesus and wanted to learn how to serve Him as prepared leaders. After two fruitful years in Balikpapan, Joiy's and Ella's Baptist leadership requested that they move to Tanjung, another majority-Islamic city, down in the southern tip of Kalimantan, and do it all over again. By that time there were four Lempases, as Tammi had been born. Again, Joiy and Ella responded by moving into an Islamic neighborhood and pastored a fledgling Baptist church in a different section of town. They served four years in that city while growing a New Testament church in the city and starting missions out in the rural areas.

For us, this unequivocally qualified them as "our own special Giants." It was one thing, for the first time, to have gone to a potentially troubled area to follow God's call, but to do it two more times after nearly being killed, goes beyond just courage. That action bespeaks of devotion and tremendous faith. And that is the stuff that makes spiritual Giants.

THE END

CPSIA information can be obtained
at www.ICGtesting.com
Printed in the USA
LVHW021717100220
646429LV00004B/315

9 781940 645650